MUSIC IN OUR HERITAGE

Our heritage is the sum total of the past. It is a record of man's achievements and failures documented by works of art and the history of nations. To each new generation, this heritage is a source of inspiration and wisdom with which to build a way of life.

Our cultural heritage is, as the word implies, an inheritance. Every citizen has an undeniable right to it, but it is not the kind of inheritance that one generation can hand over to another. You must reach out for it and claim it. Music is an important part of this heritage and a source of enjoyment that contributes to a satisfying way of life. What does music mean to you? What effect will it have on your way of life? That depends on the time and effort you spend in making the music in our heritage your own.

Music
IN OUR
HERITAGE

EMILE H. SERPOSS

IRA C. SINGLETON

Silver Burdett Company

MORRISTOWN, N. J.   CHICAGO   SAN FRANCISCO   DALLAS   ATLANTA

ACKNOWLEDGMENTS

Grateful acknowledgment is made to the following authors and publishers for permission to reprint from copyrighted materials:

American Book Company for quotations from *Discovering Music* by Howard D. McKinney and W. R. Anderson, ©1949, 1962, American Book Company, and *Music in History* by McKinney and Anderson, ©1940, 1957, American Book Company.

Lajos Bárdos for the music of *Night Bells*.

Coleman-Ross Company, Inc. for extracts from *Lexicon of Musical Invective* by Nicolas Slonimsky, ©1953, Coleman-Ross Company, Inc.

Coward-McCann, Inc. for an excerpt from *Revolt in the Arts* by Oliver M. Sayler, copyright ©1930, 1958 by Oliver M. Sayler, published by Brentano's.

Thomas Y. Crowell Company for quotations from *The Art of Music* by Beekman C. Cannon, Alvin H. Johnson, and William G. Waite, copyright 1960 by Thomas Y. Crowell Company, and *This Modern Music*, copyright 1942 by John Tasker Howard.

Crown Publishers, Inc. for quotations from *A Thing or Two About Music* by Nicolas Slonimsky, copyright 1948 by Allen, Towne & Heath, Inc.

Doubleday & Company, Inc. for quotations from *Copland on Music* by Aaron Copland, ©1960, Aaron Copland.

George G. Harrap & Company, Ltd. for the music of *Tambourine Dance (Baile de Pandero)* from *Cancionero Musical Español* by Eduardo M. Torner.

Holt, Rinehart and Winston, Inc. for excerpts from *Understanding Music* by William Fleming and Abraham Veinus, ©1958, Holt, Rinehart and Winston, Inc.

Horizon Press, Inc. for a quotation from *The Composer As Listener* by Irving Kolodin, ©1958, Horizon Press, Inc.

Alfred A. Knopf, Inc. for a quotation from *An Introduction to Music* by David D. Boyden, ©1956, Alfred A. Knopf, Inc.

Irving Kolodin for a quotation from *The Critical Composer*, published by Howell, Soskin, Inc.

Richard Leonard and Doubleday & Company, Inc. for excerpts from *The Stream of Music*, copyright 1943, Richard Anthony Leonard.

McGraw-Hill Book Company, Inc. for excerpts from *Our New Music* by Aaron Copland, copyright ©1941 by McGraw-Hill Book Company, Inc.; *America's Music* by Gilbert Chase, copyright ©1955 by Gilbert Chase; *The Concert Companion* by Robert Bagar and Louis Biancolli, copyright ©1947 by The Philharmonic Symphony Society of New York, Inc.; and *What to Listen For in Music* by Aaron Copland, copyright ©1957 by McGraw-Hill Book Co., Inc.

W. W. Norton & Company, Inc. for extracts from *The Diaries of Tchaikovsky*, translated from the Russian, with notes, by Wladimir Lakond, copyright 1945 by Wladimir Lakond; *The Enjoyment of Music* by Joseph Machlis, copyright 1955 by W. W. Norton & Company, Inc.; *From Madrigal to Modern Music* by Douglas Moore, copyright 1942 by W. W. Norton & Company, Inc.; *Music in Western Civilization* by Paul Henry Lang, copyright 1941 by W. W. Norton & Company, Inc.; *Composer and Critic* by Max Graf, copyright 1946 by W. W. Norton & Company, Inc.; *The Bach Reader*, edited by Hans T. David and Arthur Mendel, copyright 1945 by W. W. Norton & Company, Inc.

Oxford University Press for *Every Night When the Sun Goes In* from *English Folk Songs from the Southern Appalachians* by Cecil Sharp, and for a quotation from *National Music* by Ralph Vaughan Williams, ©1934, Oxford University Press.

Pantheon Books Inc. for excerpts from *Beethoven Letters, Journals and Conversations*, translated and edited by Michael Hamburger, ©1952, Pantheon Books Inc., and from *Felix Mendelssohn Letters*, edited by G. Selden-Goth, ©1945, Pantheon Books Inc.

Philosophical Library, Inc. for extracts from *The Book of Musical Documents*, edited by Paul Nettl, ©1948, Philosophical Library, Inc.

Prentice-Hall, Inc. for quotations from *The Complete Book of 20th Century Music* by David Ewen, ©1959 by Prentice-Hall, Inc., and *Listening to Music Creatively*, 2nd ed., by Edwin John Stringham, ©1959 by Prentice-Hall, Inc.

Simon and Schuster, Inc. for excerpts from *The Joy of Music* by Leonard Bernstein, copyright ©1959 by Leonard Bernstein, and *Men of Music* by Wallace Brockway and Herbert Weinstock, copyright ©1958 by Simon and Schuster, Inc.

The Society of Authors and Public Trustee for excerpts from *How to Become a Musical Critic* and *Music in London* by Bernard Shaw.

Stanford University Press for a quotation from *American Composers on American Music*, edited by Henry Cowell, ©1933, Stanford University Press.

University of Alabama Press for *I'm on My Way* from *Folksongs of Alabama* by Byron Arnold, ©1950, University of Alabama Press.

Carl Van Vechten for an excerpt from *Music After the Great War*, ©1943, Carl Van Vechten.

Collaborating editor, James W. Rooker.

The music in this book was reproduced from handwritten originals by Maxwell Weaner.

CONTENTS

Sylvie

Words and Music by
Huddie Ledbetter and Paul Campbell
Arr. by Milton Okun

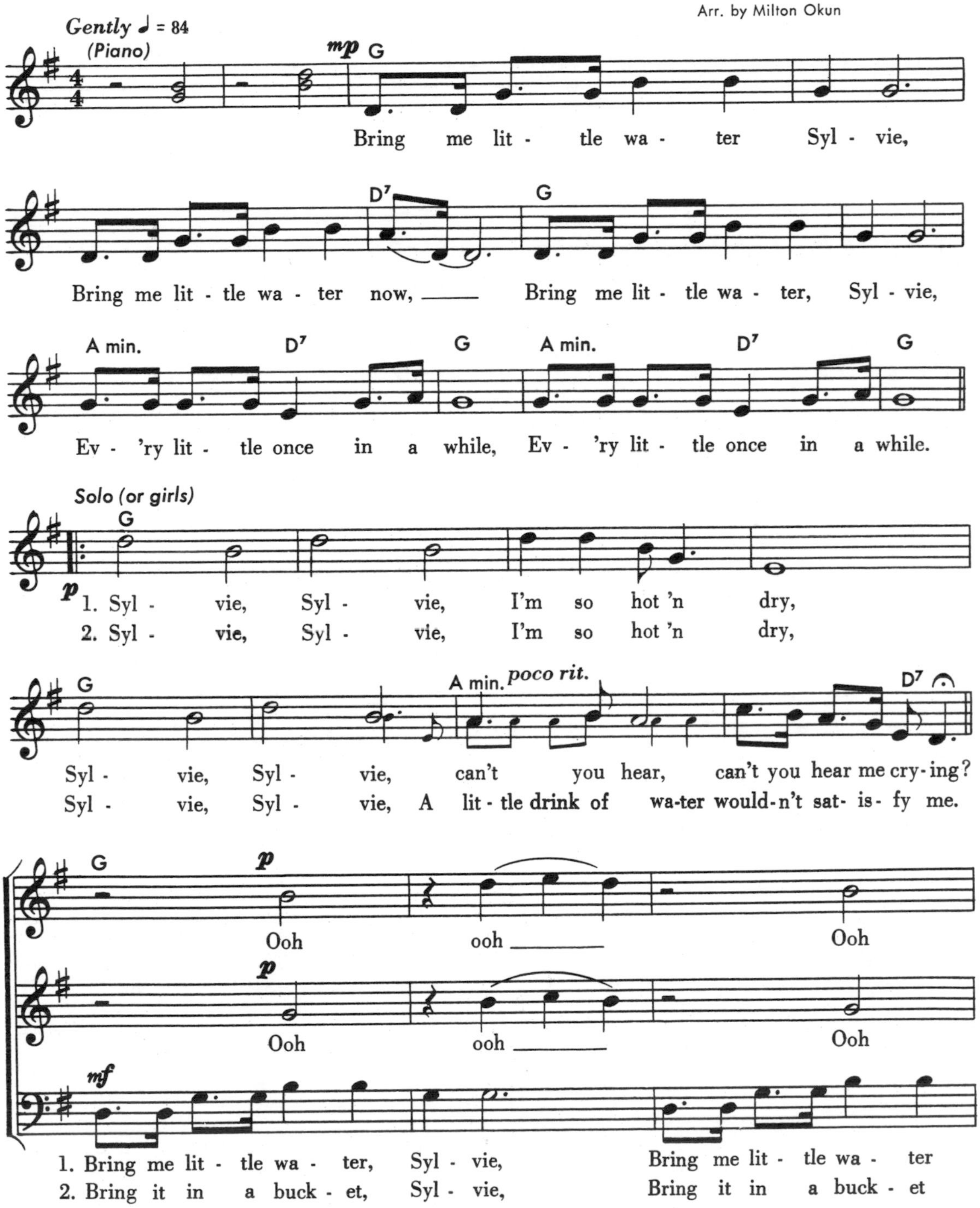

Gently ♩ = 84
(Piano)
mp
G
Bring me lit - tle wa - ter Syl - vie,
D7
G
Bring me lit - tle wa - ter now, ___ Bring me lit - tle wa - ter, Syl - vie,
A min.
D7
G
A min.
D7
G
Ev - 'ry lit - tle once in a while, Ev - 'ry lit - tle once in a while.
Solo (or girls)
G
p
1. Syl - vie, Syl - vie, I'm so hot 'n dry,
2. Syl - vie, Syl - vie, I'm so hot 'n dry,
G
A min.
poco rit.
D7
Syl - vie, Syl - vie, can't you hear, can't you hear me cry-ing?
Syl - vie, Syl - vie, A lit - tle drink of wa-ter would-n't sat- is- fy me.
G
p
Ooh ooh ___ Ooh
p
Ooh ooh ___ Ooh
mf
1. Bring me lit - tle wa - ter, Syl - vie, Bring me lit - tle wa - ter
2. Bring it in a buck - et, Syl - vie, Bring it in a buck - et

Every Night When the Sun Goes In

Appalachian Folk Song
Arr. by Milton Okun

4

Refrain

Ah _____

True love, don't weep, _____ true love, don't mourn, _____ True love, don't

Ah _____

weep, _____ true love, don't mourn. _____ True love, don't

Ah _____

weep, _____ nor mourn for me; _____ I'm go - ing a -

Ah _____

way _____ to Mar - ble - town. _____

2.

rit.

town. _____

5

All Round the Mountain

American Folk Song
Arr. by Milton Okun

me. _____

me. _____

Good Lord re - mem - ber me. _____ me. _____

Solo

1. Town gal, _____ she rides an au - to - mo - bile, ___
2. Town gal, _____ she wears a sat - in dress, _____
3. Town gal, _____ she wears __ high heel shoes, ____

Coun-try gal, _____ she rides the same, _____ **ƒ** Moun - tain
Coun-try gal, _____ she wears the same, _____ Moun - tain
Coun-try gal, _____ she wears the same, _____ Moun - tain

7

gal rides an old ox - cart, ___
gal wears a cal - i - co dress, ___
gal wears no shoes at ___ all, ___

gal rides an old ox - cart, ___ But she gets there just the
gal wears a cal - i - co dress, ___
gal wears no shoes at ___ all, ___

same. ___

All round the moun - tain, All round the moun - tain.

Lonesome Road

American Folk Song
Arr. by Milton Okun

Freely
mp

In time ♩ = 52

Hang down your head and cry, Hmmm ___ Hang your head and

mp

Look

cry.

down, look down that lone - some road, ___ Hang down your

Hang down your head and cry. _____ head and cry. The best of friends must

_____ part some-time, _____ Then why not you and I?

and I? Love, what have I done? True love, true love, what have I done _____ that you should

Ah _____ treat me so? You caused me to walk and talk with

you _____ Like I nev-er done be - fore. Hang down your head and

cry, Hmmm _____ Hang your head and cry. _____

9

Puttin' On the Style

American Folk Song
Arr. by Milton Okun

Put-tin' on the ag-o-ny, put-tin' on the style,

That's what all the young folks are do-ing all the while. And

as I look a-round me, I'm ver-y apt to smile To

see so man-y peo - ple put-tin' on the style.

Ah _____ Ah _____

Melody

(*Girls*) 1. Young man in a car-riage ___ driv-ing like ___ he's mad,

(*Boys*) 2. Sweet six - teen ___ goes to school just ___ to see the boys,

(*Girls*) 3. Young man home from col - lege ___ makes ___ a great dis - play,

Ah

With a pair of hors-es ___ he bor-rowed from his dad; He
Turns and laughs and gig-gles ___ at ev-'ry lit-tle noise; She
With a fan-cy ad-jec-tive that he can hard-ly say; It

Ah ___ Ah ___

cracks his whip so live-ly just to watch his la-dy smile, ___
turns this way a lit-tle, then ___ turns that way a-while, But
can't be found in Web-ster's, and it won't be for a while, But

D. C. al Fine

But she knows he's on-ly put-tin' on the style.
we know that she's on-ly put-tin' on the style.
ev-'ry-bod-y knows ___ he's put-tin' on the style.

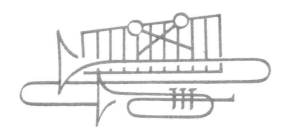

11

So Long

Words and Music by Woody Guthrie
Arr. by Milton Okun

1. I've sung this song but I'll sing it a-gain, Of the peo-ple I've met and the plac-es I've seen, Of some of the trou-bles that both-ered my mind, And a lot of good peo-ple that I've left be-hind, Say-ing:

went to your fam-'ly and asked them for you. They all said, "Take her, oh take her, please do. She can't cook or sew and she won't scrub your floor." So I put on my coat and tip-toed out the door, Say-ing:

walked down the street to the gro-cer-y store. It was crowd-ed with peo-ple, both rich and both poor. I asked the man how his but-ter was sold; He said,"One pound of but-ter for two pounds of gold." I said:

Refrain

"So long, it's been good to know you; So long, it's been good to know you; So long, it's been good to know you; It's

"So long, it's been good to know you; So long, good to know you; It's

WOODY GUTHRIE has composed more than a thousand songs. Most of them are written in the style of folk songs and, like all folk songs, tell about people and their ways of living. Guthrie calls his songs "singing history." He heard many songs while he was growing up in the town of Okemah, Oklahoma. As a young man he traveled all over the United States, learning new songs in every town he visited and writing new songs about the people he met. "So Long" is one of a group of songs Guthrie wrote during the 1930's, when most of the Southwest was turned into a "dust bowl." Although dust and gloom hung like a pall over much of the land, people managed to keep a sense of humor. This spirit is obvious in the happy lyrics and gay tune of "So Long."

Santy Anno

Sea Chanty
Arr. by Milton Okun

So heave her up and a-way we'll go, Heave a-way, ___ San-ty
An-no, ___ Heave her up and a-way we'll go, All ___
on the plains of Mex-i-co. ___

The Lonesome Dove

Kentucky Folk Song
Arr. by James W. Rooker

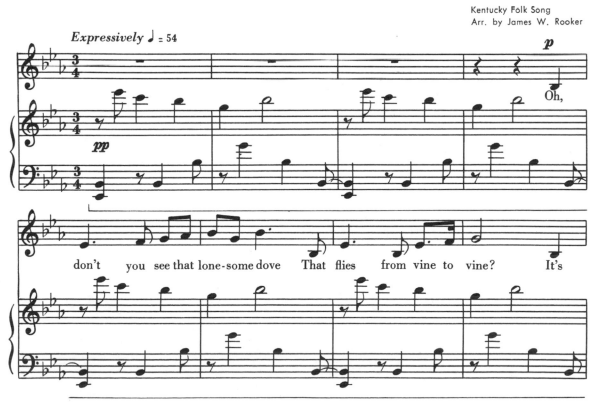

Oh, don't you see that lone-some dove That flies from vine to vine? It's

mourn - ing for its own true love, Just like I mourn for mine.

Just like I mourn for mine, my _ love, ___ Be - lieve me what I

say; ___ You are the dar-ling of my heart, Un - til my dy - ing

day. Oh, don't you see that

lonesome dove? It flies so high degree. And ain't it hard for

me to love Some-one that don't love me. Some-one that don't love

me, my love, Be-lieve me what I say; You are the dar-ling

of my heart Un-til my dy-ing day. You

are the on-ly one I love, Be-lieve me what I say; You

poco a poco rall.

are the dar-ling of my heart Un-til my dy-ing day.____

There's a Meeting Here Tonight

Spiritual
Arr. by Milton Okun

Get you read-y, There's a meet-ing here to-night, Come a-long__ there's a

meet-ing here to-night, I know you by your

dai - ly walk, There's a meet - ing here to - night.

Solo
1. Camp meet - ing in the wil - der - ness, *p* Camp
2. Come join us in the wil - der - ness, There's a meet - ing here to - night. We'll
3. We'll praise Him in the wil - der - ness, Lift

meet - ing in the wil - der - ness, *mf*
hear a - bout e - ter - nal rest, There's a meet - ing here to - night. Get you read - y,
up your voice and shout with us,

Wade in the Water

Spiritual
Arr. by Milton Okun

Slow rocking beat ♩ = 96

(Piano)
p

p Wade ____ in the wa - ter,

In the wa - ter, chil - dren,

Wade ____ in the wa - ter, chil - dren, Wade ____ in the

p

Wade in wa - ter, chil - dren, Wade in

19

Fine

wa - ter, God's a gon - na trou - ble the wa - ter. ___

wa - ter, God's a gon - na trou - ble the wa - ter. ___

Solo

1. Now Jor - dan's wa - ter is chill - y and cold, ___
2. If you ___ get there ___ be - fore ___ I do, ___

All

God's a gon - na trou - ble the wa - ter. ___

God's a gon - na trou - ble the wa - ter. ___ It chills ___ the bod - y but

Solo

Tell all ___ my friends ___ I'm

All

God's a gon - na trou - ble the wa - ter. ___

lifts ___ the soul, ___ God's a gon - na trou - ble the wa - ter. ___
com - ing too, ___ God's a gon - na trou - ble the wa - ter. ___

Balm in Gilead

Spiritual
Arr. by Milton Okun

Calmly ♩ = 72
Refrain

There __ is a balm in Gil - e - ad To
(There __ is a balm)

make the wound- ed whole; __ There __ is a balm in
(There __ is a balm)

Gil - e - ad To heal the sin - sick soul.

Fine

Solo freely

1. Some- times I feel dis - cour - aged, And think my work's in vain, But
2. You may not preach like Pe - ter, You may not pray like Paul, But

Refrain   D. S. %

then the Ho - ly Spir - it Re - vives my soul a - gain. __
you can tell the sto - ry Of One who died for all. __

There __ is a

I'm on My Way

Spiritual

Arr. by James W. Rooker

My moth - er's gone to ___ Ca - naan Land, I'm on my

rit. last time

way _____ to the Ca - naan Land, _____
go, _____ don't _ hin - der me, _____ I'm on my
gone _____ to the Ca - naan Land, _____ *rit. last time*

On my way to Ca - naan Land,
you don't go, don't hin - der me, I'm
moth - er's gone to Ca - naan Land,

1., 2. | 3.

way, praise God, to the Ca - naan Land.

way, praise God, to the Ca - naan Land. *mf* 2. If you don't Land.
f 3. My moth - er's

on my way to Ca - naan Land. *mf* 2. If Ca - naan Land.
f 3. My

23

The Babe of Bethlehem

Melody from *Southern Harmony*
Compiled by William Walker (1809–1875)
Arr. by Milton Okun

Slowly ♩. = 40

p 1. His par-ents poor in earth-ly store, to
mf 2. On the same night a glo-rious light to
3. "The cit-y's name is Beth-le-hem, in
f 4. When this was said, straight-way was made a

p 1. Hmmm hmmm Hmmm hmmm
f 4. Glo-ry glo-ry Glo-ry glo-ry

en-ter-tain the Stran-ger, They found no bed to lay His head, but
shep-herds there ap-pear-ed, Bright an-gels came in shin-ing flame, they
which God hath ap-point-ed, This glo-rious morn a Sav-ior's born, for
glo-rious sound from heav-en, Each flam-ing tongue an an-them sung, "To

hmmm hmmm Hmmm hmmm
glo-ry glo-ry Glo-ry glo-ry

(Piano)

in the ox-'s man-ger. No
saw and great-ly fear-ed. The
Him God hath a-noint-ed; By
men a Sav-ior's giv-en. In

hmmm hmmm. No
glo-ry glo-ry. "In

roy - al _ things, as used by _ kings, were seen by those _ who found _ Him. But
an - gels _ said, "Be not a - fraid, al - though we much _ a - larm _ you. We
this you'll _ know, if you will _ go, to see this lit - tle Stran - ger, His
Je - sus' _ name, the glo - ri - ous _ theme, we el - e - vate our voi - ces, At

roy - al _ things, as used by _ kings, were seen by those who found Him, But
Je - sus' _ name, the glo - ri - ous theme, we el - e - vate our voi - ces. At

a tempo

in the hay _ the Stran - ger lay, with swad - dling bands _ a - round Him. _
do ap - pear _ good news to bear, as now we will _ in - form you." _
love - ly charms _ in Mar - y's arms, both ly - ing in _ a man - ger." _
Je - sus' birth _ be peace on earth, mean-while all heav-en re - joic - es." _

in the hay the Stran - ger lay, With swad - dling bands a - round Him. _
Je - sus' birth be peace on earth, mean - while all heaven re - joic - es." _

1., 2., 3.   4.

(Piano)

Lenox

Isaac Watts (1674–1748)

Lewis Edson (1748–1820)

Strong ♩ = 112

1. Give thanks to God most high, The u - ni - ver - sal Lord, The
2. How might - y is His hand! What won - ders hath He done! He
3. Give thanks a - loud to God, To God the heav'n - ly King, And

sov - 'reign King of Kings; And be His name a - dored.
form'd the earth and seas, And spread the heav'ns a - lone.
let the spa - cious earth, His works and glo - ries sing.

1. & 3. Thy
2. His

1. & 3. Thy mer - cy, Lord, shall still en - dure, And
2. His pow'r and grace are still the same, And

1. & 3. Thy mer - cy, Lord, shall
2. His pow'r and grace are

1. & 3. Thy mer - cy, Lord, shall still en - dure, Thy mer - cy, Lord, shall
2. His pow'r and grace are still the same, His pow'r and grace are

mer - cy, Lord, shall still en - dure, Thy mer - cy, Lord, shall still en - dure, And
pow'r and grace are still the same, His pow'r and grace are still the same, And

26

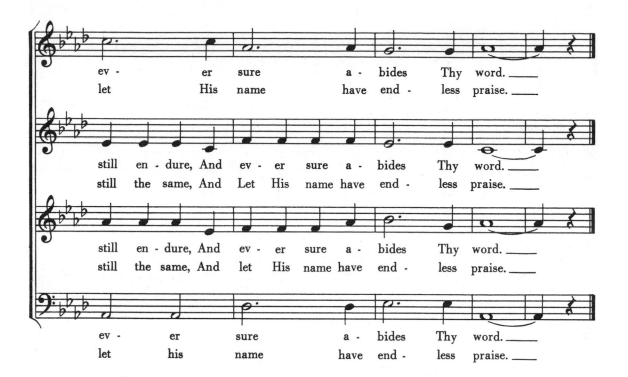

In RECENT YEARS American musicians have become interested in the choral music of early America. In hundreds of collections printed during the eighteenth and nineteenth centuries, they have discovered the works of many talented composers who played an important role in the musical life of the early settlers. Lewis Edson, the composer of "Lenox," was one of these. "Lenox" first appeared in a collection of New England hymns called *The Chorister's Companion*, published in 1782. Like many hymns of this period, "Lenox" is a part-song with the melody in the tenor part. Beginning in the middle section, it is constructed on a canon-like plan — that is, one voice following and imitating another. All voices come together in the closing measures.

Another source of early American choral music stemmed from the great religious revival that swept the American frontier at the beginning of the nineteenth century. Since few churches were large enough to hold the throngs who attended the meetings, the frontiersmen made clearings in the wilderness, erected crude benches and pulpits, and conducted services in the open. These camp meetings were characterized by impassioned preaching and energetic singing. In such an atmosphere the psalms and hymns of the established churches were out of place. As a result, a new kind of religious song sprang up, the so-called *white spiritual*. By putting religious words to familiar folk and dance tunes, the frontier preachers were able to stimulate enthusiastic singing in their services. These tunes and other hymns composed in the "folk style" were harmonized by frontier musicians. Many of the harmonizations were crude, and many of the sentiments expressed in the words seem naïve today. But these songs have a sturdy power that expresses the spirit of the people who created America. (See pages 24, 28 and 29.)

My Shepherd Will Supply My Need

Isaac Watts (1674–1748)

From *Southern Harmony*
Compiled by William Walker (1809–1875)

Sturdily ♩ = 104

1. My Shep-herd will sup-ply my need; Je - ho - vah
2. When I walk through the shades of death, Thy pres - ence
3. The sure pro - vis - ions of my God At - tend me

is His name; In pas - tures fresh He
is my stay. One word of Thy sup -
all my days. O may Thy house be

makes me feed Be - side the liv - ing stream. He
port - ing breath Drives all my tears a - way. Thy
mine a - bode And all my work be praise. There

brings my wan - d'ring spir - it back When I for -
hand in sight of all my foes Doth still my -
would I find a set - tled rest, While oth - ers

sake His ways. ___ He __ leads me __ for His
ta - ble spread, ___ My __ cup with __ bless - ings
go and come. ___ No __ more a __ stran - ger

mer - cy's __ sake In __ paths of truth and grace. ___
o - ver - flows, Thine __ oil a - noints my head. ___
or a __ guest, But __ like a child at home. ___

Canon, Four Parts in One

From *Knoxville Harmony* (1838)

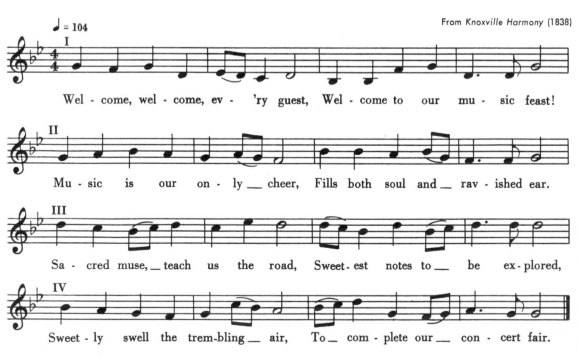

♩ = 104

I

Wel - come, wel - come, ev - 'ry guest, Wel - come to our mu - sic feast!

II

Mu - sic is our on - ly __ cheer, Fills both soul and __ rav - ished ear.

III

Sa - cred muse, __ teach us the road, Sweet - est notes to __ be ex - plored,

IV

Sweet - ly swell the trem - bling __ air, To __ com - plete our __ con - cert fair.

29

Now the Day Is Over

S. Baring-Gould (1834–1924)

Joseph Barnby (1838-1896)

Moderately ♩ = 76

p 1. Now the day is __ o - ver, Night is draw - ing __ nigh, ___
mf 2. Je - sus, give the wea - ry Calm and sweet re - pose; ___
p 3. Through the long night watch - es May thine an - gels __ spread ___
f 4. When the morn - ing wak - ens, Then may I a - rise ___

Shad - ows of the eve - ning Steal a - cross the sky.
With Thy ten - d'rest bless - ing, May our eye - lids close.
Their white wings a - bove us, Watch - ing round each bed.
Pure, and fresh, and sin - less In Thy ho - ly eyes.

eve - ning Steal a - cross the sky.
bless - ing May our eye - lids close.
bove us, Watch - ing round each bed.
sin - less In Thy ho - ly eyes.

America

Samuel Francis Smith (1808–1895)

Henry Carey (c. 1687–1743)

1. My coun - try! 'tis of thee, Sweet land of lib - er - ty,
2. My na - tive coun - try, thee, Land of the no - ble free,
3. Let mu - sic swell the breeze, And ring from all the trees
4. Our fa - thers' God, to Thee, Au - thor of lib - er - ty,

Of thee I sing; Land where my fa - thers died, Land of the
Thy name I love; I love thy rocks and rills, Thy woods and
Sweet Free - dom's song; Let mor - tal tongues a - wake, Let all that
To Thee we sing; Long may our land be bright With Free - dom's

Pil - grim's pride, From ev - 'ry moun - tain side Let free - dom ring.
tem - pled hills; My heart with rap - ture thrills Like that a - bove.
breathe par - take, Let rocks their si - lence break, The sound pro - long.
ho - ly light; Pro - tect us by Thy might, Great God, our King!

O God, Our Help in Ages Past

Isaac Watts (1674–1748)   William Croft (1678–1727)

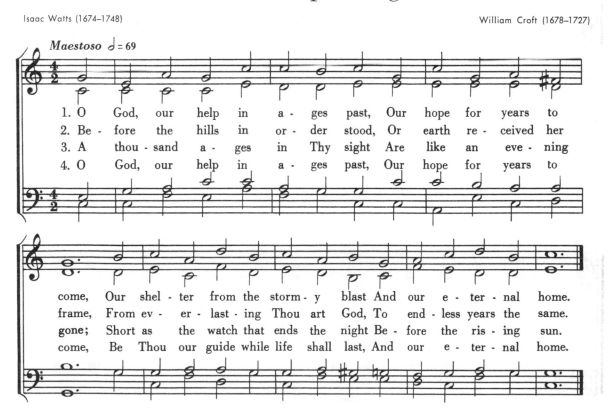

Maestoso ♩ = 69

1. O God, our help in a - ges past, Our hope for years to
2. Be - fore the hills in or - der stood, Or earth re - ceived her
3. A thou - sand a - ges in Thy sight Are like an eve - ning
4. O God, our help in a - ges past, Our hope for years to

come, Our shel - ter from the storm - y blast And our e - ter - nal home.
frame, From ev - er - last - ing Thou art God, To end - less years the same.
gone; Short as the watch that ends the night Be - fore the ris - ing sun.
come, Be Thou our guide while life shall last, And our e - ter - nal home.

31

The Star-Spangled Banner

Francis Scott Key (1779–1843)

John Stafford Smith (c. 1750–1836)

1. O__ say! can you see, __ by the dawn's ear - ly light, What so
2. On the shore dim - ly seen __ through the mists of the deep, Where the
3. O __ thus be it ev - er when __ free men shall stand Be -

proud - ly we hailed at the twi - light's last gleam - ing? Whose broad
foe's haugh - ty host in dread si - lence re - pos - es, What is
tween their loved homes and the war's des - o - la - tion! Blest with

stripes and bright stars, through the per - il - ous fight, O'er the
that which the breeze, o'er the tow - er - ing steep, As it
vic - t'ry and peace, may the heav'n res - cued land Praise the

ram - parts we watched, were so gal - lant - ly stream - ing! And the
fit - ful - ly blows, half con - ceals, half dis - clos - es? Now it
Pow'r that hath made and pre - served us a na - tion. Then __

rock - ets' red glare, the bombs burst - ing in air, Gave ____
catch - es the gleam of the morn - ing's first beam, In full
con - quer we must, when our cause it is just, And ____

proof through the night ____ that our flag was still there.
glo - ry re - flect - ed now ____ shines on the stream;
this be our mot - to: "In ____ God is our trust!"

O ____ say, does that ____ Star - Span - gled Ban - ner ____ yet ____ wave ____
'Tis the Star - Span - gled ____ Ban - ner, O long may ____ it ____ wave ___
And the Star - Span - gled ____ Ban - ner, in tri - umph shall ____ wave ___

O'er the land ____ of the free and the home of the brave?
O'er the land ____ of the free and the home of the brave!
O'er the land ____ of the free and the home of the brave!

Bonnie Doon

Robert Burns (1759–1796)

Scottish Melody
Arr. by James W. Rooker

thorn; _____ Ye _____ mind me o' _____ de - part - ed joys, _____ De-
tree; _____ but _____ my fause lov - er stole _____ my rose. _____ But

part- ed nev - er to _____ re - turn. _____
ah! _____ he left the thorn _____ wi' me. _____

Blow the Wind Southerly

Northumbrian Folk Song
Arr. by James W. Rooker

Smoothly ♩. = 44

Blow the wind south - er - ly,

Blow south - er - ly, blow south - er - ly, blow south - er - ly,

Blow south - er - ly, blow south - er - ly, blow south - er - ly,

Blow south - er - ly, blow south - er - ly, blow south - er - ly,

south - er - ly, south - er - ly, Blow the wind south o'er the bon - ny blue sea;

blow south - er - ly, blow south - er - ly, blow, blow. _____

blow south - er - ly, blow south - er - ly, blow, blow. _____

Blow the wind south-er-ly, south-er-ly, south-er-ly, Blow bon-ny breeze __ my

Blow wind south o'er the sea. South-er-ly

Blow wind south o'er the sea. South-er-ly

lov-er to me. 1. They told me last night there were ships in the off-ing, And
2. I stood by the light-house that last time we part-ed, Till

wind blow. Ah

wind blow. Ah

I hur-ried down to the deep roll-ing sea; But my eye could not see it, wher-
dark-ness came down o'er the deep roll-ing sea; And no long-er I saw the bright

But my eye could not see it, wher-
And no long-er I saw the bright

But my eye could not see it, wher-
And no long-er I saw the bright

Ah

36

ev - er might be it, The bark that is bear-ing my lov-er to me.
bark of my lov - er. Blow bon - ny breeze ___ and bring him to me.

ev - er might be it, The bark that comes to me.
bark of my lov - er. Blow my love to me.

ev - er might be it, The bark that is com - ing to me.
bark of my lov - er Blow bon - ny breeze ___ to me.

The bark that comes to me.
___ Blow my love to me.

slower

Blow the wind south - er - ly, south - er - ly, south - er - ly,

Blow south - er - ly, blow south - er - ly,

Blow south - er - ly, blow south - er - ly,

rit.

Blow bon - ny breeze ___ my lov - er to me.

blow south - er - ly wind blow.

blow south - er - ly wind ___ blow.

Kitty Magee

Irish Folk Song
Arr. by Harold Kidder

Masters in This Hall

William Morris (1834–1896)

French Folk Song
Arr. by Milton Okun

Joyfully ♩. = 112

1. Mas - ters in this hall, _____ Hear the news to-day, _____

Brought from o - ver sea _____ And ev - er I you pray:

Refrain

No - el! No - el! No - el! No - el sing we clear!
No - el! No - el! No - el! No - el sing we loud!

No - el! No - el! No - el! No - el sing we clear! Hol - pen
No - el! No - el! No - el! No - el sing we loud! God to -

1.

are all folk on earth;_ Born_ is God's Son so dear.
day hath poor folk rais-ed and _

2.

cast a-down the proud.

mf

2. Go - ing o'er the hills, _____ Through the milk - white snow, _____
3. Then to Beth - 'lem town _____ We went two and two, _____ And

p

Ah _____

Heard I ewes____ bleat _____ While the wind did blow.
in a sor - ry place _____ Heard the ox - en low.

Ah _____ While the wind did
Heard the ox - en

Refrain
No - el! No - el! No - el! No - el sing we clear! Hol - pen

blow.
low.
No - el! No - el! No - el! No - el sing we

are all folk on earth;___ Born___ is God's Son so dear.

clear! _____ Is God's Son so dear, God's Son so

No - el! No - el! No - el! No - el sing we loud! God to -

dear. No - el! No - el! No - el! No - el sing we

day hath poor folk rais - ed and ___ cast a - down the proud.

loud! _____ Cast a - down the proud.

4. This is Christ the Lord, _____ Mas - ters, be ye glad! _____

Christ - mas is come in, _____ And no folks should be sad.

No - el! No - el! No - el! No - el sing we clear!

This is Christ the Lord, _____ Mas - ters, be ye glad! _____

No - el! No - el! No - el! No - el sing we clear!

Christ - mas is come in _____ And no folks should be sad.

Refrain

No - el! No - el! No - el! No - el sing we loud! God to -

No - el! No - el! No - el! Sing we

day hath poor folk rais - ed and _____ cast a - down the proud.

loud, _____ Cast a - down the proud.

Greensleeves

16th-Century English Ballad
Arr. by Emile Serposs

With an easy swing ♩. = 52

(Piano)

Hmmm _____

A - las, my love, ___ you do me wrong ___ to
I have been read - y at your hand ___ to

Hmmm _____

cast me off ___ dis - cour - teous - ly, And I have lov - ed
grant what - ev - er you would crave. I have both wag - ed

you too long, ___ De - light - ing in ___ your com - pa - ny.
life and land, ___ Your love ___ and good - will for to have.

Refrain

f Green - sleeves ___ is all my joy, ___ Green - sleeves ___ is

Green - sleeves, Green -

my de-light; _pp_ Green- sleeves is my heart of gold___ And

sleeves, Hmmm _____

rit. last time

who but my La-dy Green- sleeves.

Auprès de ma blonde

French Folk Song
Arr. by Milton Okun

With an easy swing ♩. = 116

Refrain

G D⁷ G D⁷ G

_f_

Au - près de ma blon - de, qu'il fait bon, fait bon, fait bon,

G D⁷ G D⁷ G

Au - près de ma blon - de, qu'il fait bon, fait bon. ___ Fait

_mf_

1. Au
2. La
3. Ell'

_p_

bon, fait bon, fait bon, fait bon, fait bon. Fait

44

Artsa alinu [Homeland]

English version by Ruth Martin

Israeli Folk Song
Arr. by Milton Okun

Spirited ♩ = 132

Here on our own land, Dear, cher-ished home-land, Our hearts and hopes are

Ar-tsa a-li-nu, Ar-tsa a-li-nu, Ar-tsa a-li-

set. Here on our own land, Dear, cher-ished home-land,

nu. Ar-tsa a-li-nu, Ar-tsa a-li-nu,

nu, A-li-nu. Ar-tsa a-li-nu, Ar-tsa a-li-nu,

Our hearts and hopes are set. Though we've done the plow-ing and sow-ing,

Ar-tsa a-li-nu. K'var cha rash-nu v'-gam za-ra-nu,

Seen the fields start bloom-ing and grow-ing, We have not reaped our

K'var cha rash-nu v'-gam za-ra-nu. A-val od lo ka-

Seen the fields start bloom-ing and grow-ing, We have

K'var cha rash-nu v'-gam za-ra-nu. Od lo,

own yet, We have not reaped our own yet,
tsar - nu, *A - val od lo ka - tsar - nu,*

not reaped our own yet, We have not reaped our own yet,
od lo ka - tsar - nu, *Od lo,* *od lo ka - tsar - nu,*

We have not reaped our own yet, We have not reaped our own yet.
A - val - od lo ka - tsar - nu, *A - val od lo ka - tsar - nu.*

We have not reaped our own yet, We have not reaped our own yet.
A - val od lo ka - tsar - nu, *A - val od lo ka - tsar - nu.*

A la claire Fontaine [At the Fountain]

English version by Ruth Martin

French Canadian Folk Song
Arr. by James W. Rooker

Smoothly ♩ = 42

(Piano)

p

1. Just as the sun is set-ting, Cast- ing its part-ing ray,
1. *A la clai - re fon - tai - ne M'en al - lant pro - men - ner,*

p Hmmm _____ Hmmm _____

46

2. I pause beside the fountain
   Watching its shining play,
   Thinking of how we met there
   First on a summer day.

2. *Sous les feuilles d'un chêne*
   Je me suis fait sécher.
   Sur la plus haute branche
   Le rossignol chantait.

3. Sun made a hundred rainbows
   Gleam in the fountain spray.
   I filled your arms with flowers,
   Love's ever dear bouquet.

3. *Chante, rossignol, chante,*
   Toi qui as le coeur gai;
   Tu as le coeur à rire,
   Moi je l'ai-t-à pleurer.

4. Hearts filled with soaring gladness,
   We had no words to say.
   Gone is that golden moment
   Time could not hold nor stay.

4. *J'ai perdu ma maîtresse*
   Sans l'avoir mérité,
   Pour un bouquet de roses
   Que je lui refusai.

My Joy Would Grow in Measure

English words by Ruth Martin

15th-Century German Folk Song
Arr. by Harold Kidder

Lively ♩ = 112

(He) 1. My joy would grow in meas-ure If for-tune smiled on me And
(She) 2. My heart has al-ways not-ed You are in love with me. More
(He) 3. From ev-'ry-where a-round me Your good-ness seems to shine, And

let me once know pleas-ure, From pain and sor-row free. I have but one en-
ten-der and de-vot-ed No friend could ev-er be. I'm hon-ored by the
if your fa-vor found me, What joy would then be mine! My hopes would be re-

deav-or, To win you for my wife And cher-ish you for-
yearn-ing, The love that you ex-press. Such prais-es mer-it
quit-ed, My heart would sing your praise! At last we'd dwell u-

Reproduced above is "My Joy Would Grow in Measure" (*Mein freud möcht sich wohl mehren*) as it appeared in the original manuscript of the *Locheimer Liederbuch,* a fifteenth-century collection of German songs. A portion of the text is shown beneath the musical notation.

Angelique—O

English words by Margaret Marks

Haitian Folk Song
Arr. by Milton Okun

Rhythmically ♩ = 72

mp

Go home, lit-tle girl, go home, lit-tle girl, You're too young to wed.

Melody **mf**

An -

Go home, lit-tle girl, go home, lit-tle girl, You're too young to wed.

ge-lique - O, ___ An - ge-lique - O, ___ Go home to your ma -

pp

Go home, lit-tle girl, go home, lit-tle girl, You're too young to

ma! An - ge-lique - O, ___ An - ge-lique - O, ___

wed. Go home, lit-tle girl, go home, lit-tle girl,

Go home to your pa-pa! An - ge-lique-O, ___ An - ge-lique-O, ___

p

You're too young to wed. Ah ___

Me Gustan Todas [I'm Fond of All Girls]

Spanish Folk Song
Arr. by Milton Okun

English version by Ruth Martin

la la la la la la. Ah ____

ru - bia me gus - ta más. La la la la la, La la la
yon - der with gold - en hair.

Ah ____ Ah ____

la la, La la la la la la la la, La la la la la la, la la la la

La la la la la la la.

la la, La la la la la la la la la.

Tambourine Dance

English words by Ruth Martin

Spanish Folk Song
Arr. by Milton Okun

Strongly accented ♩ = 120

1. Lis - ten to my tam-bou - rine now, Hear it sing-ing of ro - mance,____
2. Lis - ten to my tam-bou - rine now, It is sad as sad can be; ____

Hear it sing - ing of ro - mance. _____
It is sad as sad can be; _____

Lads, it's tell - ing you to hur - ry, Choose your part-ner for the dance,____
For my love, my fa - v'rite part - ner Is not here to dance with me, ____

Choose your part- ner for the dance: _____
Is not here to dance with me: _____

Ai - la-la- la, Ai - la-la- la, Ai - la- la, La - la,

Ai - la-la- la, Ai - la- la- la. ____

56

Laredo

Mexican Folk Song
Arr. by Milton Okun

English version by Ruth Martin

Slowly ♩ = 54

(Piano) *p* lightly

mp

I'm go - ing up - on a
Ya me voy, pa - ra el La -

Melody

jour - ney, my love, I've come here to say fare - well. In La -
re - do, mi bien, Te ven - go á de - cir a - diós. De a -

re - do I'll long for you, my love, Far more than my words can
llá te man - do de - cir, mi bien, Co - mo se man - cuer - nan

tell. *mf* To o - pen my heart's own se - crets, my love, I
dos. To - ma e - sa lla - vi - ta de o - ro, mi bien, Ab -

give you this gold-en key. So un-lock it and you will

re mi pe-cho y ver-ás: Lo__ mu-cho que yo te

see, my love, Just how much you mean to me.

quie-ro, mi bien, Y_el mal pa-go que me dás.

I

To-ma

La la la la la la la la la.

give you this box of treas-ures, my love, And

e - sa ca - ji-ta de o - ro, mi bien, Mi -

La la la la la la la la la.

ev - 'ry - thing it con - tains. Just un -

ra lo que lle - va_den - tro. Lle -

La la la la la la la la la. La la la la la la la

lock it and you will find, __ my love, Life's pleas-ures and joys and

va_a_mo - res, lle - va ce - los, mi bien, y un po - co de sen - ti - mien -

58

la.
pains.   I'm go-ing up-on a jour-ney, my love, I've
to.   *Ya me voy, pa-ra el La-re-do, mi bien, Te*

come here to say fare-well.   In La-re-do I'll long for
ven-go á de-cir a-diós.   De a-llá te man-do de-

you, _ my love, Far more than my words can tell. _____
cir, _ mi bien, Co-mo se man-cuer-nan dos. _____

A GREAT QUANTITY and a wide variety of songs exist in Mexico today — religious songs, dance songs, love songs. Many authorities say that the most unique musical form heard in Mexico today is the *corrido* (plural, *corridos*), a type of narrative folk ballad. It is said that one way of knowing a people is to listen to their songs. Much may be learned about the nature and character of the people in rural Mexico by studying the subject matter treated in a personal, matter-of-fact manner in the corridos. These songs tell of heroes and bandits, of revolutions and local politics, as well as personal emotions and feelings.

"Laredo" is a love song. Mexican love songs almost automatically bring to mind a handsome caballero with a guitar serenading his sweetheart on a beautiful moonlit night. If a young man's musical talents are limited, he hires a group of professional singers to serenade her. These serenades are known as *gallos*. They are always accompanied by a guitar, and each one begins with a traditional song of greeting and ends appropriately with a song of farewell. "Laredo" is an important theme in Aaron Copland's *El Salón México* (page 194).

Henrietta's Wedding

Words and Music by
Joseph Marais and Albert Diggenhof
Arr. by Milton Okun

be? When will it be? _____ We've been in-vit-ed — to

When will it be?

Hen-ri-et-ta's wed-ding, — Though she can't tell — us when it — will

be.

ff (Piano)

We've been in-

We've been in-vit-ed!

vit-ed — to Hen-ri-et-ta's wed-ding, — And we want to — know

Where will it be?

where it — will be. _____ We won-der which way — to go to — the

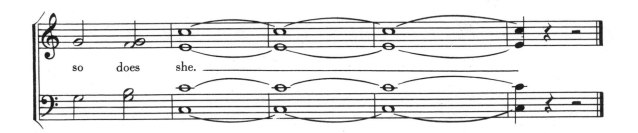

so does she. _____

Johnny's My Boy

Ghana Folk Song
Counter Melodies by Max V. Exner

John - ny's my boy, I sent him to school to

learn how to spell John Bull, John - ny, John - ny, John - ny.

Counter Melodies

1.

John - ny, John - ny, John - ny, ___ John - ny, John - ny, John - ny, ___

2.

John - ny, ___ John - ny, John - ny, ___ John - ny, ___ John - ny, John - ny. ___

3.

John - ny's my boy, ___ and I sent him to school ___ for to

learn how to spell ___ John - ny Bull; ___ John - ny!

Play throughout
Small Drum

Large Drum

Dear Love, Now I Must Leave Thee

HEINRICH ISAAC (c. 1450–1517) was one of the most prolific and versatile composers of the fifteenth century. One of his best-known compositions is "Innsbruck, I Must Leave Thee." This song, first printed in 1539, is a composition for four voices based on an old folk melody. Many settings of Isaac's original song may be found in music literature. For example, "Dear Love, Now I Must Leave Thee" is an adaptation made by Leonhard Lechner in 1577. "The Whole World Lies in Shadows" (page 66), one of Johann Sebastian Bach's most moving chorales, is also based on Isaac's song. Other settings of this song are found in modern hymn books.

English words by Ruth Martin

Heinrich Isaac (c. 1450–1517)
Arr. by Leonhard Lechner (c. 1550–1606)

65

The Whole World Lies in Shadows

Paulus Gerhardt (1607–1676)
English version by Ruth Martin

Heinrich Isaac (c. 1450–1517)
Harmonized by J. S. Bach (1685–1750)

1. The whole world lies _ in shad - ows, The _ sleep-ing woods and mead - ows; All
2. O sun, where have _ you van - ished? Your _ glo - ry has been ban - ished By
3. And when the day _ is o - ver The _ bright stars _ shine _ and hov - er A -
1. Nun ru - hen al - le Wäl - der, Vieh, Men-schen, Städt und Fel - der, es

men and beasts are still. My soul, be up and do - - ing, Thy _
night, the foe of day. But go in peace, un - know - - ing The _
loft in Heav - en's blue. What joy will then be - fall me The _
schläft die gan - ze Welt; ihr a - ber, mei - ne Sin - - nen, auf, _

Mas - ter's steps pur - su - - ing; Ac - com - plish thy Cre - a - tor's will.
light of God is glow - - ing And shows my heart its lone - ly way.
day my God will call me To dwell _ a - - mong them, too.
auf, ihr sollt be - gin - - nen, was eu - rem Schöp - fer wohl - ge - fällt.

THE EVOLUTION of the *chorale* started with Martin Luther (1483–1546) during the early part of the sixteenth century. This musical form was used for
congregational singing in the German Lutheran church. Present-day musicians, however, are most familiar with chorales as they were used and harmonized by Bach. The four-voice setting above is one of nine harmonizations
Bach made of this old melody.

Mass VII: KYRIE

The texture of music may be compared with the texture of cloth. Both are composed of separate threads woven together to create a particular pattern. *Melody* may be called the horizontal thread; *harmony*, the vertical thread.

An interesting comparison may be made of the musical textures of the hymn "O God, Our Help in Ages Past" (page 31) and Lotti's "Kyrie." In the hymn, there is a melody line (soprano part) supported by a chordal accompaniment. The main emphasis in this musical texture is vertical. In "Kyrie," however, *each* voice part is an independent melody. The musical texture of this composition is the result of four melodic lines sounding simultaneously. The main emphasis here is horizontal. The difference in the over-all effect of these compositions is due in part to the difference in the *texture* of each.

From the Liturgy of the Church

Antonio Lotti (c. 1667–1740)

le - - - i - son, _____ e le - - - i - son.

son, e - le - - - - - - - i - son.

le - - i - son, e - le - - i - son.

le - - - - - - - - - i - son.

Chri - ste e - le - - - i - son, e - le -

Chri - ste e le - - i - son, e - le -

Chri - ste e - le - - - - i - son, e - -

- - - - i - son, e - le - -

- - i - son, e - le - - i - son, _____

Chri - ste e - le - - - i - son, e -

Tod und Schlaf [Death and Sleep]

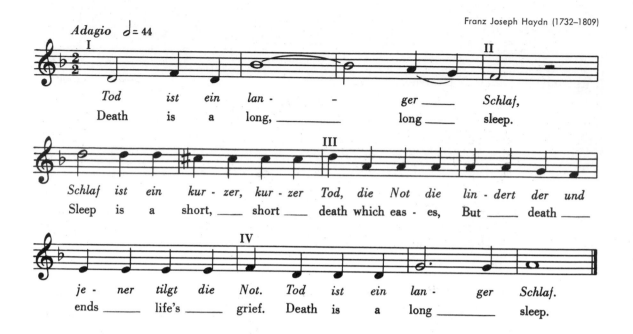

Franz Joseph Haydn (1732–1809)

Adagio ♩ = 44

I Tod ist ein lan - ger ___ Schlaf,
   Death is a long, ___ long ___ sleep.

III Schlaf ist ein kur - zer, kur - zer Tod, die Not die lin - dert der und
     Sleep is a short, ___ short ___ death which eas - es, But ___ death ___

IV je - ner tilgt die Not. Tod ist ein lan - ger Schlaf.
    ends ___ life's ___ grief. Death is a long ___ sleep.

THE *round* and *canon* are musical forms that evolved during the thirteenth and fourteenth centuries. It is important to understand these forms because they represent two of the oldest kinds of part-music in our musical heritage. The word "canon" comes from a Greek word meaning "rule." A canon, therefore, is a musical composition written strictly according to rule. This type of composition is one in which all parts have the same melody throughout, but the parts follow one another at different time intervals. In this follow-the-leader process, one voice imitates the other, beginning one or more beats later and beginning on the *same* or a *different* pitch level. In a round, the process is similar. The voice parts follow one another at different time intervals, but the voices always begin on the *same* pitch as the leader.

The strict rules of canon writing have challenged the skill of composers for centuries. Haydn and Mozart were no exceptions. We know of forty-two canons by Haydn and thirty-five by Mozart. Learning to write canons is just one step in learning the craft of musical composition.

Kanon

English words by Ruth Martin

Wolfgang Amadeus Mozart (1756–1791)

With spirit ♩ = 132

Friends, for - get the cares that bore us, Come and join the jol - ly

cho - rus! A song of praise, to hap - py days! Let us be mer - ry one and

all! You sit so i - dly in your plac - es With gloom - y looks up - on your

fac - es. Come on, re - joice And raise your voice To hap - py days—A song of

praise, a song of praise! Are you like don - keys far too old to bray? Are you like

don - keys far too old to bray? Sing out, sing out, Sing out now one and

all; Laugh and be gay! We toast ro - mance and

joy - ous song! May they sur - round us all life long! Long live,

long live, Long live ro - mance and song!

Ich liebe dich [I Love You]

DURING THE LATTER PART of the Middle Ages (c. 1100) the Troubadours of southern France and their German counterparts, the Minnesingers, initiated the first great era of secular song. The songs of these early poet-musicians represent the first step in the development of the *art song*, a form of musical expression that reached artistic perfection eight hundred years later in the songs of Franz Schubert (see "Sea Calm," page 75). Schubert believed that a song should express a deep-felt emotion through the perfect unity of words and music. In other words, the mood of the music must correspond to the mood of the words. The lyric poetry of Goethe (1749–1832), Schiller (1759–1805), and Heine (1797–1856) inspired German composers to write the kind of song that resulted in a golden age of song. By the early nineteenth century, German song commanded such a special place in the musical literature of the world that the term *lied* (plural, *lieder*) was accepted in other languages as the term designating "art song." The original title of the Beethoven art song below was "Zartliche Liebe" (Tender Love).

Carl F. W. Herrosee (1754-1821)
English version by Ruth Martin

Ludwig van Beethoven (1770–1827)

My love be-longs to you a-lone As yours is mine to
Ich lie - be dich, so wie du mich, am A - bend und am

treas - ure. To - geth - er we have shared and known Life's sor - row and_ its_
*Mor - gen, noch_ war kein Tag, wo du und ich nicht theil - ten uns'- re_*

pleas - ure.
Sor - gen.

Love__ eased the woes we
Auch__ wa - ren sie für

had to bear, And__ blos-somed in__ our__ keep - ing. You brought me com - fort
dich und mich ge - theilt leicht zu er - tra - gen; du trö - stet-est im

in de - spair And__ I con - soled your weep - ing, con - soled your
Kum - mer mich, ich __ weint' in dei - ne Kla - gen, in die - ne

weep - ing. I__ pray Al-might -y God a - bove To spare you and to
Kla - gen. Drum__ Got - tes Se - gen ü - ber dir, du mei - nes Le - bens

guide ____ you. May ____ He pro - tect and bless our love And let me dwell ____ be -
Freu - de, Gott ____ schü - tze dich, er - halt' dich mir, schütz' und er - halt' ____ uns ____

side you. May He pro - tect and bless our love And
bei - de, Gott schü - tze dich, er - halt' dich mir, schütz'

let me dwell be - side you. And let me dwell be - side you, In
und er - halt' uns bei - de, er - halt', er - halt, uns bei - de, er -

joy be - side _____ you.
halt' uns bei - - de.

74

Meeres-Stille [Sea Calm]

Johann Wolfgang von Goethe (1749–1832)
English version by Ruth Martin

Franz Schubert (1797–1828)

Still - ness reigns up - on the wa - ter, Ly - ing calm with -
Tie - fe Stil - le herrscht im Was - ser, oh - ne Re - gung

out a breeze, And the anx - ious, watch - ful sail - or
ruht das Meer, und be - küm - mert sieht der Schif - fer

Scans the end - less, glass - y seas. Not a breath of
glat - te Flä - che rings um - her. Kei - ne Luft von

wind or mo-tion, Death-like si-lence, strange and drear,
kein-er Sei-te, To-des-stil-le fürch-ter-lich:

And the fear-some might-y o-cean, Brood-ing, wave-less, far and near.
in der un-ge-heu-ern Wei-te re-get kei-ne Wel-le sich.

The Sea

William Dean Howells (1837–1920)

Edward MacDowell (1861–1908)

Broadly, with rhythmic swing   ♩. = 58

One sails__ a-way to__ sea, to__ sea, One stands on the shore__ and

cries;___ The ship___ goes down the world and___ the light___ On the sul - len wa - ter dies.___ The whis - per-ing shell___ is mute,___ And aft - er is e - vil cheer;___ She shall stand on the shore___ and cry in vain, in vain, Man - y and man - y a year.___ But the state - ly wide-winged

THE COMPOSER Edward MacDowell was at his best as a "poet of nature." In his music he was able to capture the moods of the forest, the fields, and the ocean. A majority of critics consider "The Sea" one of the finest of Mac-Dowell's forty-two songs. One eminent critic has called it the strongest song of the sea since Schubert's "Am Meer" (By the Sea). MacDowell believed that in an art song the piano accompaniment should always support the voice part as well as enhance the poetic idea contained in the words. An interesting comparison may be drawn between the accompaniment of this song, which suggests the rolling of the ship on the seas, and the somber, expressive chords that Schubert used in the accompaniment of "Sea Calm" (see page 75).

Ein Ton [One Tone]

PETER CORNELIUS pursued the tradition of German lied begun by Franz Schubert (1797–1828). He is probably remembered best for his art song "Ein Ton" (One Tone), a unique composition that keeps the voice part on one tone throughout while the accompaniment sustains all the melodic interest. The words of "Ein Ton" are Cornelius' own — he was a gifted poet as well as musician. In this song, the music and words are so interwoven that one without the other would be incomplete.

Peter Cornelius
English version by Ruth Martin

Peter Cornelius (1824-1874)

I hear a tone of won-drous kind Re-sound-ing
Mir klingt ein Ton so wun-der-bar In Herz und

in my heart and mind. _____ Is it your
Sin-nen im-mer-dar. _____ Ist es der

Ev - er be - side me as I weep, Sing-ing my an-guished grief to sleep.

Als stie - gest lie - bend nie - der du Und säng-est mei - nen Schmerz in Ruh!

Christmas Oratorio: PRAISE YE THE LORD OF HOSTS

THE ORATORIO became established as a musical form in the seventeenth century. This distinctive form of church music grew out of the sacred operas that were popular in Italy during the last half of the sixteenth century. The oratorio, in the modern sense of the word, is largely the creation of George Frederick Handel (1685–1759). In fact, Handel's *Messiah* is probably the best-known oratorio ever written.

In many respects oratorio is similar to *opera*. Both may contain a variety of recitatives (from the Latin *recitare*, meaning "to recite"), arias, small ensembles, choruses, and instrumental pieces. However, unlike opera, oratorio is usually based on a biblical text, and there is no scenery or costumes. Also, the chorus takes a position of greater importance in oratorio than it does in opera.

Nathan Haskell Dole (1852–1935)

Camille Saint-Saëns (1835–1921)

Maestoso ♩ = 108

f Praise ye the Lord of hosts, sing His sal - va - tion,

f Praise ye the Lord of hosts, sing His sal - va - tion,

bless His name, show forth His praise in His ho - ly house!

bless His name, show forth His praise in His ho - ly house!

ia, _____ Al - le - lu - ia, Al - le - lu - ia, _____

Ale - le - lu - ia, Al - le - lu - ia, Al - le - lu - ia, _____

ia, Al - le - lu - ia, Al - le - lu -

Al - le - lu ia, Al - le - lu - ia, Al - le - lu - ia, Al - le - lu -

___ Al - le - lu - ia, Al - le - lu - ia. *ff* Re - joice, ye

___ Al - le - lu - ia, Al - le - lu - ia. *ff* Re - joice, ye

ia, Al - le - lu - ia, Al - le - lu - ia.

ia, Al - le - lu - ia, Ale - le - lu - ia.

an - gels, re - joice, all ye na - tions, now in the face of the

an - gels, re - joice, all ye na - tions, for He com -

84

Lord, for He com - eth. Al - le - lu - ia.

eth. Al - le - lu - ia, Al - le - lu - ia.

Requiem: PIE JESU

English words by Ruth Martin

Gabriel Fauré (1845–1924)

Adagio ♩ = 44
dolce

Pi - e Je - su Do - mi - ne, do - na e - is
Gen - tle Je - sus, ev - er blest, Grant their souls e -

re - qui - em; do - na e - is re - qui - em.
ter - nal rest, Grant their souls e - ter - nal rest.

p
Pi - e Je - su
When their mor - tal

mf
Do - mi - ne, do - na e - is re - qui - em;
sor - rows cease, May the faith - ful rest in peace,

do - na __ e - is re - qui em.
May __ the __ faith - ful rest in peace.

dolce
Do - na, __ do - na, Do - mi - ne,
For - ev - er - more, O Lord Di - vine,

poco cresc.
do - na e - is re - qui em; sem - pi - ter - nam
May Thy light up - on them shine. Lord of mer - cy,

p
re - qui - em, sem - pi - ter - nam re - qui - em,
God a - bove, Let them know Thy bound - less love,

pp sem - pi - ter - nam re - qui - em. *mf* Pi - e, pi - e
Let them know Thy bound - less love. Gen - tle Je - sus,

Je - su, pi - e __ Je - su Do - mi - ne,
ev - er blest, Grant __ their __ souls e - ter - nal rest.

do - na __ e - is, do - na e - is sem - pi - ter - nam
May __ the __ faith - ful, May __ the __ faith - ful, When their mor - tal

poco rit.
re - qui - em, sem - pi - ter - nam re - qui - em.
sor - rows cease, Rest for - ev - er - more in peace.

Night Bells

English words by Ruth Martin

Lajos Bárdos

Tranquillo ♩ = 56

p

After the evening sun has descended Night draws a veil and

Day is done.

daytime is ended. Through the fragrant wood a gentle

Through the wood a

breeze is sighing, Stirring grass and leaves to whisper

breeze is sighing, Stirring grass and

low, replying. Down in the valley church bells are ringing,
Bim - bom, Bim - bom,

leaves replying. Bom.

Young and Old

AROUND THE BEGINNING of the twentieth century a new development took place in musical composition. At that time many composers were breaking away from the old traditions and were beginning to experiment with new ways of using the materials of music. As a result, much of the music written in the early 1900's sounded strange to the average listener. Because this "new music" was difficult to understand, a wide gap occurred between the composer and the listening public. Paul Hindemith, one of the great composers of the twentieth century, felt it was necessary to bring the modern composer and his listeners closer together. To achieve this goal, he originated Gebrauchsmusik, a type of composition that introduced modern music to amateurs and beginning musicians. The German word *Gebrauchsmusik*, translated literally, means "music for use." It was Hindemith's idea to supply the public with worthwhile music written in the modern style and with a minimum of technical difficulty, so that the amateur could perform the "new music" and learn something about it. One of his best-known pieces of Gebrauchsmusik is "We Build a City," a musical game for children. Other modern composers have written music with a specific purpose in mind. For example, Aaron Copland (1900–   ), one of America's great composers, wrote "The Second Hurricane," a "play-opera" for high school performance. Kurt Weill (1900–1950), a German composer who came to America, wrote "Down in the Valley" specifically for college students. This is a folk opera based on American folk tunes. The part-song "Young and Old" is one of nine songs Hindemith composed for Silver Burdett Company for use in its music textbooks.

Charles Kingsley (1819–1875)   Paul Hindemith

hey   for   boot   and   horse, lad,   And round the world _____ a - way;
(the world)

Young blood must have ___ its course, lad,   And ev - ery dog   his day.

Slow and soft ♩ = 60

2. When all   the world is   old,   lad,   And   all   the trees __ are brown; And

all   the   sport   is   stale,   lad,   And all the wheels __ run   down; Creep

home and take your place there, The   spent and maimed ___ a - mong;   God

grant you   find   one __ face there,   You loved when   all   was   young.

The Bartered Bride: OPENING CHORUS

English words by Ruth Martin

Friedrich Smetana (1824–1884)

See the bud - ding flow - ers __ spring - ing, __ Hear the soar - ing sky - lark __ sing - ing! Joy and sun - shine far and near, __ far and near, Now that love - ly spring is here, spring is here!

Now that love - ly spring is here, __ spring is here!

Though young hearts are swift - ly___ cap - tured In this

fair and sun - ny___ sea - son, Though young hearts are

swift - ly___ cap - tured In this fair and sun - ny___

sea - son, Do not give your word___ for - ev - er Till you

look on love___ with___ rea - son!

Andrea Chenier: PARTING CHORUS

THE DRAMATIC EVENTS of the French Revolution (1789–1799) have provided rich source material for many novelists, dramatists, and composers. The most notable example in operatic literature is "Andrea Chenier," by the Italian composer Umberto Giordano (1867–1948). Although the plot of Giordano's opera is fictitious, the title character is a historical figure who achieved considerable reputation as a poet in the last decade of the eighteenth century. Chenier was sympathetic to the revolutionary cause, but he was denounced by the more determined revolutionary leaders because of his outspoken criticism of their policies. As a result, he was imprisoned and later was sent to the guillotine without a trial. In general, the plot of the opera follows the events of Chenier's life.

The opening scene of the opera is set in the luxurious ballroom of a château in Paris, where elegantly dressed members of the nobility have gathered for a reception and entertainment. Part of the entertainment is provided by a group of musicians, dressed as shepherds and shepherdesses, who sing the "Parting" Chorus as an accompaniment to a ballet pantomime. At the conclusion of the entertainment Chenier reads his latest poem. Then, to the surprise and displeasure of his audience, he denounces them for thinking only of their own pleasure and comfort while most of the people in Paris are forced to live in abject poverty. At the end of the first act Chenier leaves to join the revolutionaries.

Luigi Illica (1857–1919)
English version by Ruth Martin

Umberto Giordano (1867–1948)

Andantino grazioso ♩ = 80

Dear friends, we part to-mor-row, To-mor-row, to-mor-row; _____ To shores ___ un-known and lone-ly We jour-ney with-

O Pa-sto-relle, ad-di-o, ad-di-o, ad-di-o! _____ Ci av-via-mo ver-so li-di i-gno-ti e

Madama Butterfly: HUMMING CHORUS

Giacomo Puccini (1858–1924)

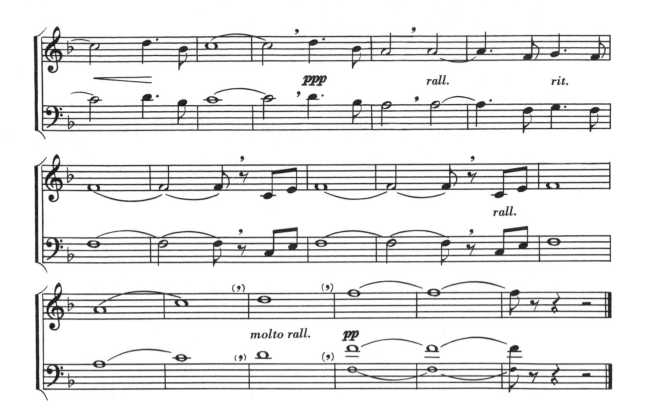

Madame Butterfly was one of the most successful plays produced in 1900. It was written by David Belasco, a well-known American playwright and theatrical producer. Puccini saw Belasco's play in London and recognized its operatic possibilities at once. He immediately began work on *Madama Butterfly*, which is one of the best-loved operas in music literature.

Puccini makes skillful use of Japanese melodies to create an appropriate musical background for the story of Lieutenant Pinkerton, an American naval officer who marries a young Japanese girl while on a tour of duty in Japan. One of the most poignant moments in the opera occurs at the end of the second act. From her house situated high on a hill overlooking the harbor of Yokohama, Cio Cio San (Madama Butterfly) sights Pinkerton's ship returning to Japan after an absence of three years. As night falls, the motionless figures of Cio Cio San, her small son, and her faithful attendant Suzuki are seen silhouetted against the window as they wait for Pinkerton. The "Humming" Chorus is the off-stage musical accompaniment to this moving scene.

97

Songs that Swept America, 1850-1905

THE SONGS on the following pages are not the only ones that swept America between 1850 and 1905, but they are representative of those that survive today. Every generation since the middle of the 1800's has been exposed to hundreds of songs whose melodies and lyrics captured the public imagination. Most of them rose to sudden popularity and then were forgotten just as quickly. A few "popular" songs from every decade pass the test of time. These become a distinctive part of our musical heritage.

The span of fifty-five years represented by the songs in this section was an important period in the history of American music. It was during this time that American music for entertainment began to find a voice of its own. Instead of copying European music-hall tunes, song writers made use of the fascinating variety of musical characteristics found in the folk songs of national groups that were pouring into the United States. Songs began to have a new sound — an American sound. The popular song became a national fad, and the foundation was laid for the big business of popular music.

Popular music exists today in many forms — songs from Broadway shows, jazz in all its varieties, and commercial music written to satisfy the ever-changing tastes of an ever-changing population. Variety and change were just as typical of popular music in the early days. As you sing this sampling of the old songs, you will also notice some characteristics that remind you of popular music today — syncopation, an emphasis on an offbeat, a sentiment that is familiar. This music still satisfies the only demand made of popular songs — they must be fun to sing.

Nelly Bly-1850

Words and Music by
Stephen C. Foster
Arr. by James W. Rooker

Cheerfully ♩=108
(Piano)

repeat ad lib.

mf
1. Nel - ly Bly! Nel - ly Bly! Bring the broom a - long. We'll
2. Nel - ly Bly! has a voice Like a tur - tle dove, I
3. Nel - ly Bly! Nel - ly Bly! Nev - er, nev - er sigh,

sweep the kitch - en clean, my dear, And have a lit - tle song.
hear it in the mead - ow and I hear it in the grove.
Nev - er bring a tear - drop to the cor - ner of your eye. For the

Poke the wood, my la - dy love, And make the fire burn, And
Nel - ly Bly has a heart Warm as a cup of tea, And
pie is made of pump - kins And the mush is made of corn, And there's

while I take the ban - jo down, Just give the mush a turn.
big - ger than the sweet po - ta - to Down in Ten - nes - see.
corn and pump - kins plen - ty, love, A - ly - ing in the barn.

Refrain

f Hey, Nel - ly! Ho, Nel - ly! Lis - ten, love, to me; I'll

Hey, Nel - ly! Ho! Lis - ten, love, to me;

sing for you, play for you A dul- cem mel - o - dy.

Sing for you a dul- cem mel - o - dy, my Nel - ly.

Hey, Nel - ly! Ho, Nel - ly! Lis - ten, love, to me; I'll

Hey, Nel - ly! Ho! Lis - ten, love, to me;

1.,2. D. S. 3.

sing for you, play for you A dul- cem mel - o - dy. dy.

Sing for you a dul- cem mel - o - dy. dy.

There's Music in the Air - 1854

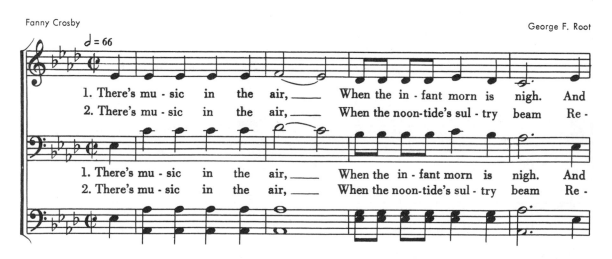

Fanny Crosby

George F. Root

♩ = 66

1. There's mu - sic in the air, ____ When the in - fant morn is nigh. And
2. There's mu - sic in the air, ____ When the noon - tide's sul - try beam Re -

1. There's mu - sic in the air, ____ When the in - fant morn is nigh. And
2. There's mu - sic in the air, ____ When the noon - tide's sul - try beam Re -

100

faint its blush is seen _____ On the bright and laugh-ing sky.
flects a gold-en light _____ On the dis-tant moun-tain stream.

faint its blush is seen _____ On the bright and laugh-ing sky.
flects a gold-en light _____ On the dis-tant moun-tain stream.

Many a harp's ec-stat-ic sound Thrills us with its joy pro-found,
When be-neath some grate-ful shade Sor-row's ach-ing head is laid,

Many a harp's ec-stat-ic sound Thrills us with its joy pro-found,
When be-neath some grate-ful shade Sor-row's ach-ing head is laid,

While we list, en-chant-ed there To the mu-sic in the air.
Sweet-ly to the spir-it there Comes the mu-sic in the air.

While we list, en-chant-ed there To the mu-sic in the air.
Sweet-ly to the spir-it there Comes the mu-sic in the air.

101

When Johnny Comes Marching Home-1863

Words and Music by
Patrick S. Gilmore
Arr. by James W. Rooker

1. When

John - ny comes march - ing home a - gain, Hur - rah! _____ Hur -
love __ and friend - ship on that day, Hur - rah! _____ Hur -
read - y for the ju - bi - lee, Hur - rah! _____ Hur -

rah! _____ We'll give him a heart - y wel - come then, Hur -
rah! _____ Their choic - est treas - ures then dis - play, Hur -
rah! _____ We'll give __ the he - roes three times three, Hur -

rah! _____ Hur - rah! _____ The __ men will cheer, __ the
rah! _____ Hur - rah! _____ And __ let each one __ per -
rah! _____ Hur - rah! _____ The __ lau - rel wreath __ is

boys will shout, The la - dies they __ will all turn out, And we'll
form some part, To fill with joy __ the war - rior's heart, And we'll
ready - y now To place up - on __ his loy - al brow, And we'll

all feel gay when John - ny comes march - ing
all feel gay when John - ny comes march - ing
all feel gay when John - ny comes march - ing

1.,2.

home! _____
home! _____

3.

2. Let
3. Get

home! _____

In the Gloaming - 1877

Meta Orred

Annie F. Harrison
Arr. by James W. Rooker

Quietly ♩ = 69

p

1. In the gloam-ing, oh, my dar-ling, When the lights are dim and low,
2. In the gloam-ing, oh, my dar-ling, Think not bit-ter-ly of me,

And the qui-et shad-ows fall-ing Soft-ly come and soft-ly go;
Though I passed a-way in si-lence, Left you lone-ly, set you free.

When the winds are sob-bing faint-ly With a gen-tle un-known woe
For my heart was crushed with long-ing; What had been could nev-er be.

Will you think of me and love me As you did once long a-go?
It was best to leave you thus, dear, Best for you and best for me.

While Strolling Through the Park - 1884

Words and Music by
Ed Haley
Arr. by Frank Scott

Cheerfully ♩=56
Sand blocks

Ah

While stroll - ing through the park one day, _____ In the

Ah

Ah

mer - ry, mer - ry month of May, _____ I was tak - en by sur - prise, by a

Ah _____ Ah _____ Ah

pair of ro-guish eyes, In a mo - ment my poor heart was stole a - way. _____ A

Ah _____ (Whistle)

smile was all she gave to me. (Whistle)

Of course, we were as hap-py as can be,

(Whistle)

(Whistle) Ah! I im-me-di-ate-ly raised my hat, ___ And

fin-al-ly ___ she re - marked, ___ I ___ nev-er shall for-get that ___

love - ly aft-er-noon, I ___ met her at the foun-tain in the park. in the park.

Hello, My Baby-1899

Ida Emerson

Joe Howard
Arr. by James W. Rooker

Lively ♩ = 100

(Piano)

Hel - lo, my ba - by, Hel - lo, my hon - ey,

Hel - lo, my rag - time gal! Send me a kiss by

wire; Ba - by, my heart's on fire!

If you re - fuse me, Hon - ey, you'll lose me, Then you'll be left a -

lone; Oh, ba - by, Tel - e - phone and tell me I'm your

1.
own.

2.
own.

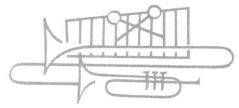

In the Good Old Summer Time-1902

Ren Shields

George Evans
Arr. by Frank Scott

Smoothly ♩.= 63

In the good old sum - mer time, _____ In the good old

In the good old sum - mer time, _____ In the good old

Sum - mer time, good old

sum - mer time, _____ Stroll - ing thro' the shad - y

sum - mer time, _____ Stroll - ing thro' the shad - y

sum - mer time, _____ Stroll - ing thro' the shad - y

lanes With your ba - by mine. _____ You hold her

lanes With your ba - by mine. _____ You hold her

lanes, ba - by mine, ba - by mine. You hold her

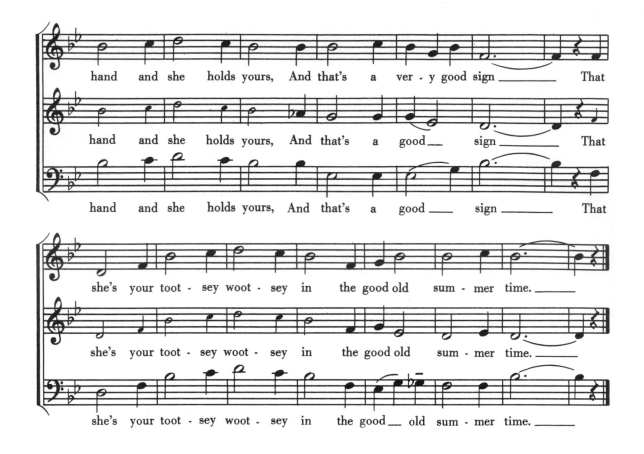

hand and she holds yours, And that's a ver-y good sign _____ That

hand and she holds yours, And that's a good _____ sign _____ That

hand and she holds yours, And that's a good _____ sign _____ That

she's your toot-sey woot-sey in the good old sum-mer time. _____

she's your toot-sey woot-sey in the good old sum-mer time. _____

she's your toot-sey woot-sey in the good _____ old sum-mer time. _____

Wait Till the Sun Shines, Nellie-1905

Andrew Sterling

Harry von Tilzer
Arr. by James W. Rooker

Smoothly ♩ = 88 ; **Detached** ♩ = 132

Wait till the sun shines, Nel-lie, When the

clouds go drift-ing by. We will be hap-py,

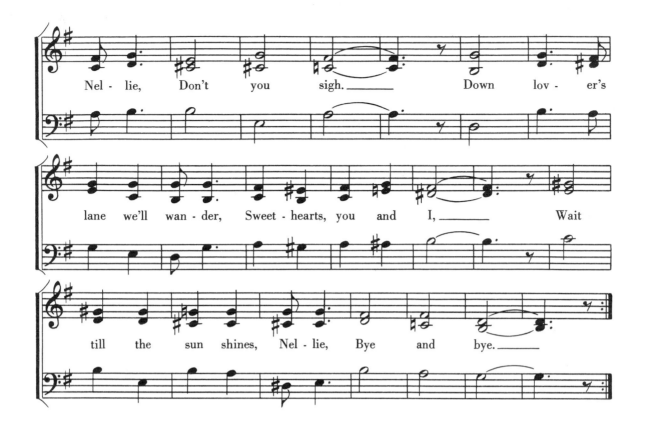

Nel - lie, Don't you sigh._____ Down lov - er's

lane we'll wan - der, Sweet - hearts, you and I,_____ Wait

till the sun shines, Nel - lie, Bye and bye._____

Mary's a Grand Old Name - 1905

from the musical production *Forty-five Minutes from Broadway*

Words and Music by
George M. Cohan
Arr. by James W. Rooker

Soft shoe tempo ♩ = 88

(Piano)

For it is Mar - y,

Doo doo doo doo doo doo doo doo doo doo

Mar - y, plain as an - y name can be;_____ But with pro-

doo *continue throughout*

pri - e - ty, so - ci - e - ty will say, "Ma -

rie." _____ But it was Mar - y, Mar - y,

long be-fore the fash - ions came, _____ And there is some - thing there that

1. sounds so square, It's a grand old name. 2. For it is name.

Give My Regards to Broadway -1904

from the musical production *Little Johnny Jones*

Words and Music by
George M. Cohan

March tempo ♩ = 126

f

(Piano)

Give my re - gards to

Broad - way, Re - mem - ber me to Her - ald

Square, _____ Tell all the gang at For - ty - Sec - ond Street that I will soon be there; _____ Whis - per of how I'm yearn - ing To min - gle with the old time throng, _____ Give my re - gards to old Broad - way And say that I'll be there ere

1. long. _____
2. long. _____

Hey, Look Me Over

from the musical production *Wildcat*

Carolyn Leigh

Cy Coleman
Arr. by James W. Rooker

113

How can you win the world, if no-bod-y knows you're there.

Kid, when you need the crowd, the tick-ets are hard to sell;

Still you can lead the crowd, if you can get up and yell:

D. S. %

BROADWAY is one of the most famous streets in the world. The name *Broadway* applies not only to the street itself but to a whole area surrounding it between 41st Street and 57th Street. More than seventy-five theaters are located in this section of mid-town Manhattan. Ablaze with lights at night, it is a scene of noisy crowds and traffic jams. At one time or another it has been the working address of nearly every great star of stage and screen. It is the birthplace and home of that unique American contribution to theatrical art, the Broadway musical.

What is a Broadway musical? Its full name is "musical comedy," although some Broadway musicals are not comedies at all. Fundamentally, it is a play set to music, but so is Puccini's *Madama Butterfly*. However, no one would mistake a Broadway musical such as *Wildcat* for an Italian opera. The music of *Wildcat* is in the style of that typically American product, the popular song. The plot deals with oil prospecting in the West. The time is the early 1900's. The action and settings are realistic. The songs and dances are used to carry the story forward, not inserted for their own sake. Finally, the dialogue, instead of being sung throughout, combines spoken and sung lines.

In its development through the years, the Broadway musical has borrowed ideas from opera, minstrel shows, vaudeville, and variety shows. Yet it has an identity of its own. As a form of theater it seems to be moving toward the artistic unity of opera. One thing is certain: as long as musical productions from Broadway include songs that become hit tunes, they will be called musicals rather than operas — no matter what they actually are.

Ole Buttermilk Sky

Words and Music by
Hoagy Carmichael and Jack Brooks
Arr. by James W. Rooker

ques - tion, that ques - tion, "Do you, dar - lin', do you do?" It - 'll be

eas - y, so eas - y If I can on - ly bank on you. Ole but-ter-milk

pp Ooh

sky, I'm tell - ing you why; now you know. Keep it in

Ooh *f* Ole but - ter - milk

mind to - night, Keep a - brush-ing those clouds from sight. Hang a moon a - bove her

sky, Don't you fail me when I'm need - in' you most.

hitch - ing post; Hitch me to the one I love. You can if you

mf

MUSIC HAS BEEN closely identified with motion pictures ever since some silent-picture director discovered that music played on the set helped the actors give better performances. In those days every motion-picture theater was equipped with a piano or an organ on which a musician would improvise "mood music" to accompany the silent images on the screen.

With the advent of sound movies, it was discovered that although the dialogue could now be heard, filmed performances still needed background music to a greater degree than did live performances on the legitimate stage. Hollywood began to furnish employment for a great number of musicians — composers, arrangers, instrumentalists, singers, copyists, and conductors. Hollywood musicals became popular and remain so to the present day. The Academy of Motion Picture Arts and Sciences annually awards "Oscars" for the best background score and the best featured song.

Hoagy Carmichael and Jack Brooks have both written extensively for motion pictures. Carmichael received an Academy Award in 1951 for his song "In the Cool, Cool, Cool of the Evening," and "Ole Buttermilk Sky" has won an Oscar nomination.

Music by Jack Brooks has been used in such movies as *Harvey, Summer Stock, Witness for the Prosecution,* and *Mexican Hayride.*

Put On a Happy Face

from the musical production *Bye Bye Birdie*

Lee Adams

Charles Strouse
Arr. by James W. Rooker

Gray skies are gon-na clear up, ___ Put on a hap-py face;

Brush off the clouds and cheer up, ___ Put on a hap-py face.

Take off the gloom-y mask of trag-e-dy, It's not your style;

You'll look so good that you'll be glad ya' de-cid-ed to smile! ___

Pick out a pleas-ant out-look, ___ Stick out that no-ble chin;

Wipe off that "full of doubt" look, ___ Slap on a hap-py grin! And

spread sun - shine all o - ver the place, Just

put on a hap - py face! face! _____

A BROADWAY MUSICAL represents the combined efforts of many people — a producer who finances the production, a director, a set and costume designer, lighting and sound technicians, stage crew, a choreographer, actors, actresses, an author, a composer, and a lyricist. On opening night the talent, money, and time of all these people crystallize in a three-hour performance.

When *Bye Bye Birdie* opened on April 14, 1960, Broadway acclaimed its newest and youngest hit song writing team, Charles Strouse, who wrote the music, and Lee Adams, who wrote the lyrics. Only after working together for thirteen years had Strouse and Adams experienced the kind of fame that comes from collaborating on a successful Broadway musical.

Strouse and Adams follow a pattern for writing a song. In their first discussion, as Adams describes it, "We may wind up with only a title or maybe just the 'pulse' of a scene, but we do get the feeling of what we want. Then I leave and go home. I generally work at night . . . it may take as long as a week of sitting, thinking, and working. Then I bring my words to Charles. We'll work them over together and then he takes over. He's up at six a.m. each day to start working. After he gets the tune, we work together on both words and music, and I've got to admit that the dummy tunes and meters I use when writing the lyrics often differ greatly from Charles's music, but I've learned to re-think."

Strouse, a native New Yorker, entered the Eastman School of Music at the age of fifteen. At graduation in 1947, he was awarded two scholarships to Tanglewood, where he studied under Aaron Copland and had many of his works performed. He has also studied with David Diamond and with Nadia Boulanger, France's leading teacher of composition.

Adams, a graduate of the School of Journalism of Columbia University, has always been interested in writing lyrics. He wrote a college show, *Howdy, Stranger*, while attending Ohio State University. When Adams and Strouse first started to work together, Adams continued to write for radio and to do editorial work for magazines.

The background of these two young men points up the fact that there is no quick and easy way to lasting success in the field of professional music. Both men have had excellent training plus years of experience in practicing their craft. In addition, Strouse and Adams have the imagination to create works that stand out in the highly competitive world of Broadway.

Sentimental Journey

Words and Music by
Bud Green, Les Brown, Ben Homer
Arr. by James W. Rooker

Gon - na take a sen - ti - men - tal jour-ney, Gon - na set my
Got my bag, I got my res - er - va-tion, Spent each dime I

heart at ease, ___ Gon - na make a sen - ti - men - tal jour-ney
could af - ford. ___ Like a child in wild an - tic - i - pa - tion,

To re - new old mem - o - ries. ___
Long to hear that "All a - board." ___

Sev - en, ___

that's the time we leave, at sev - en. ___ I'll be wait - in' up for

Heav - en, ___ Count - in' ev - 'ry mile of rail - road track ___ that takes me back. ___ *mf* Nev - er thought my heart could be so "yearn - y." Why did I de - cide to roam? ___ Got - ta take this sen - ti - men - tal jour - ney, Sen - ti - men - tal jour - ney home. ___ Sen - ti - men - tal ___ jour - ney home. ___

JOHANN SEBASTIAN BACH

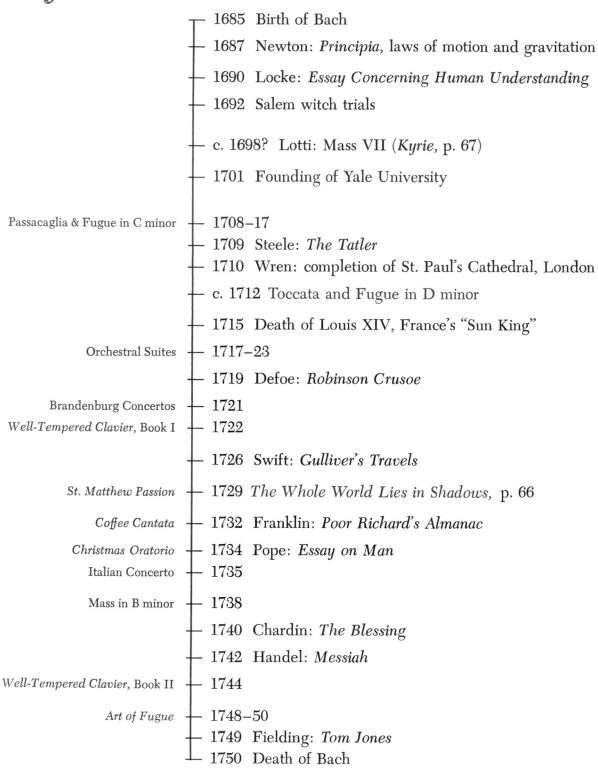

	1685	Birth of Bach
	1687	Newton: *Principia,* laws of motion and gravitation
	1690	Locke: *Essay Concerning Human Understanding*
	1692	Salem witch trials
	c. 1698?	Lotti: Mass VII (*Kyrie,* p. 67)
	1701	Founding of Yale University
Passacaglia & Fugue in C minor	1708–17	
	1709	Steele: *The Tatler*
	1710	Wren: completion of St. Paul's Cathedral, London
	c. 1712	Toccata and Fugue in D minor
	1715	Death of Louis XIV, France's "Sun King"
Orchestral Suites	1717–23	
	1719	Defoe: *Robinson Crusoe*
Brandenburg Concertos	1721	
Well-Tempered Clavier, Book I	1722	
	1726	Swift: *Gulliver's Travels*
St. Matthew Passion	1729	*The Whole World Lies in Shadows,* p. 66
Coffee Cantata	1732	Franklin: *Poor Richard's Almanac*
Christmas Oratorio	1734	Pope: *Essay on Man*
Italian Concerto	1735	
Mass in B minor	1738	
	1740	Chardin: *The Blessing*
	1742	Handel: *Messiah*
Well-Tempered Clavier, Book II	1744	
Art of Fugue	1748–50	
	1749	Fielding: *Tom Jones*
	1750	Death of Bach

SCORED FOR LISTENING

Johann Sebastian Bach
Toccata and Fugue in D minor

124

126

SCORED FOR SINGING

Johann Sebastian Bach

Toccata and Fugue in D minor: Toccata, Measures 137–143

WOLFGANG AMADEUS MOZART

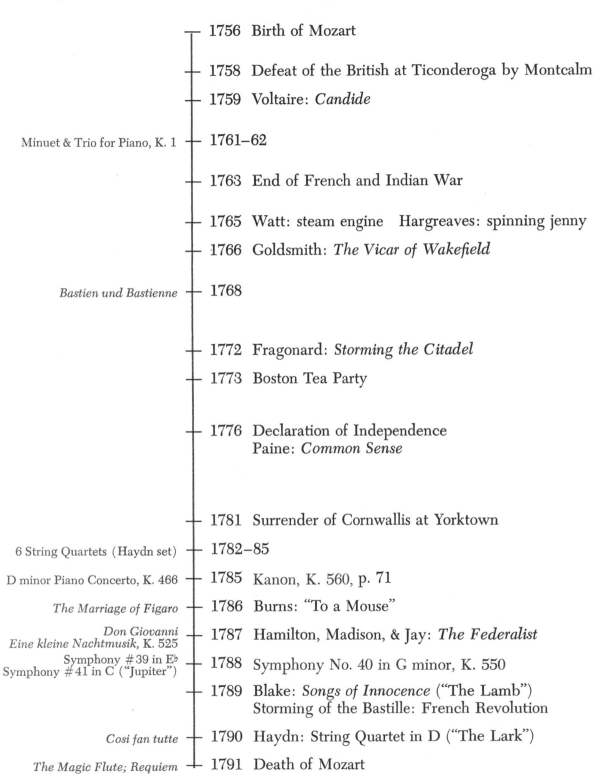

	1756	Birth of Mozart
	1758	Defeat of the British at Ticonderoga by Montcalm
	1759	Voltaire: *Candide*
Minuet & Trio for Piano, K. 1	1761–62	
	1763	End of French and Indian War
	1765	Watt: steam engine Hargreaves: spinning jenny
	1766	Goldsmith: *The Vicar of Wakefield*
Bastien und Bastienne	1768	
	1772	Fragonard: *Storming the Citadel*
	1773	Boston Tea Party
	1776	Declaration of Independence Paine: *Common Sense*
	1781	Surrender of Cornwallis at Yorktown
6 String Quartets (Haydn set)	1782–85	
D minor Piano Concerto, K. 466	1785	Kanon, K. 560, p. 71
The Marriage of Figaro	1786	Burns: "To a Mouse"
Don Giovanni *Eine kleine Nachtmusik*, K. 525	1787	Hamilton, Madison, & Jay: *The Federalist*
Symphony #39 in E♭ Symphony #41 in C ("Jupiter")	1788	Symphony No. 40 in G minor, K. 550
	1789	Blake: *Songs of Innocence* ("The Lamb") Storming of the Bastille: French Revolution
Cosi fan tutte	1790	Haydn: String Quartet in D ("The Lark")
The Magic Flute; Requiem	1791	Death of Mozart

SCORED FOR LISTENING

Wolfgang Amadeus Mozart
Symphony No. 40 in G minor, K. 550: Movement 1

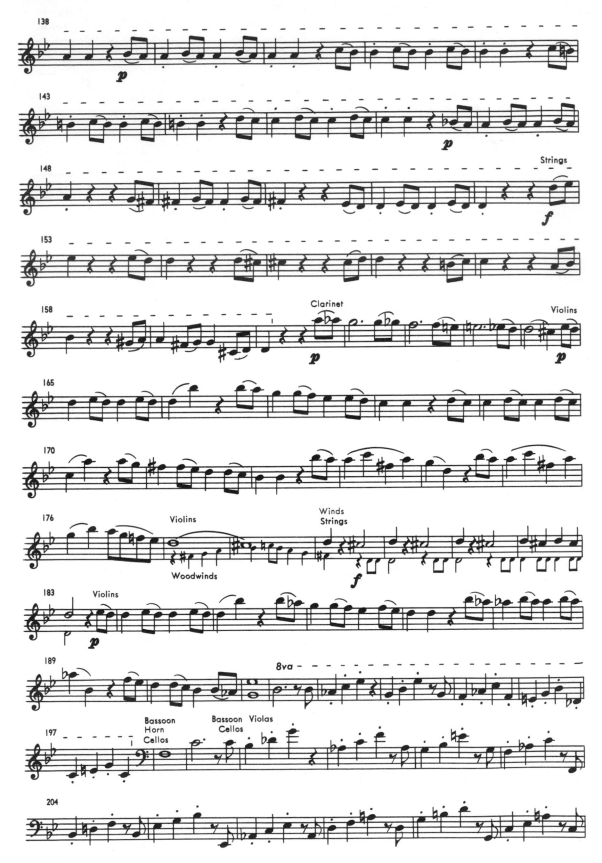

132

SCORED FOR SINGING

Wolfgang Amadeus Mozart

Symphony No. 40 in G minor, K. 550: Movement 1, Measures 211–225

LUDWIG VAN BEETHOVEN

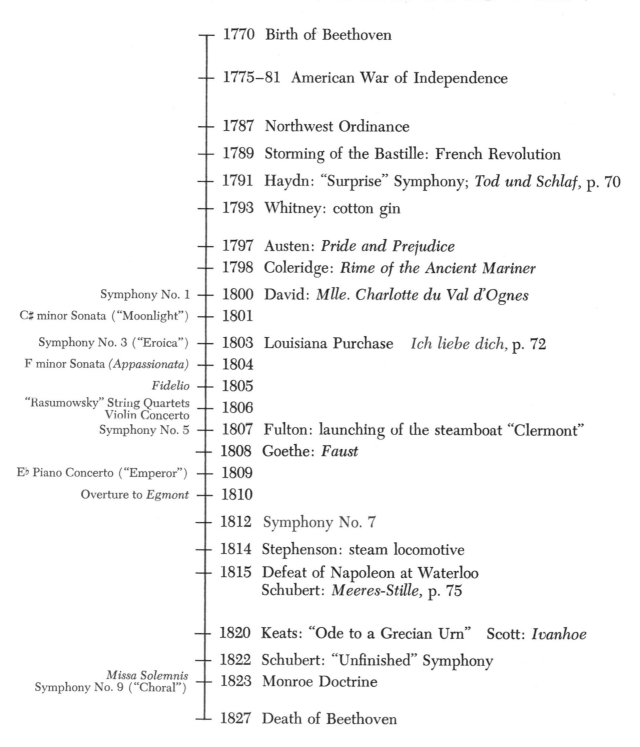

	1770	Birth of Beethoven
	1775–81	American War of Independence
	1787	Northwest Ordinance
	1789	Storming of the Bastille: French Revolution
	1791	Haydn: "Surprise" Symphony; *Tod und Schlaf,* p. 70
	1793	Whitney: cotton gin
	1797	Austen: *Pride and Prejudice*
	1798	Coleridge: *Rime of the Ancient Mariner*
Symphony No. 1	1800	David: *Mlle. Charlotte du Val d'Ognes*
C♯ minor Sonata ("Moonlight")	1801	
Symphony No. 3 ("Eroica")	1803	Louisiana Purchase *Ich liebe dich,* p. 72
F minor Sonata (*Appassionata*)	1804	
Fidelio	1805	
"Rasumowsky" String Quartets Violin Concerto	1806	
Symphony No. 5	1807	Fulton: launching of the steamboat "Clermont"
	1808	Goethe: *Faust*
E♭ Piano Concerto ("Emperor")	1809	
Overture to *Egmont*	1810	
	1812	Symphony No. 7
	1814	Stephenson: steam locomotive
	1815	Defeat of Napoleon at Waterloo Schubert: *Meeres-Stille,* p. 75
	1820	Keats: "Ode to a Grecian Urn" Scott: *Ivanhoe*
	1822	Schubert: "Unfinished" Symphony
Missa Solemnis Symphony No. 9 ("Choral")	1823	Monroe Doctrine
	1827	Death of Beethoven

SCORED FOR LISTENING

Ludwig van Beethoven
Symphony No. 7 in A, Op. 92: Movement 2

137

138

SCORED FOR SINGING

Ludwig van Beethoven

Symphony No. 7 in A, Op. 92: Movement 2, Measures 1–24 and 25–32

Measures 1–24

Measures 25–32

140

RICHARD WAGNER

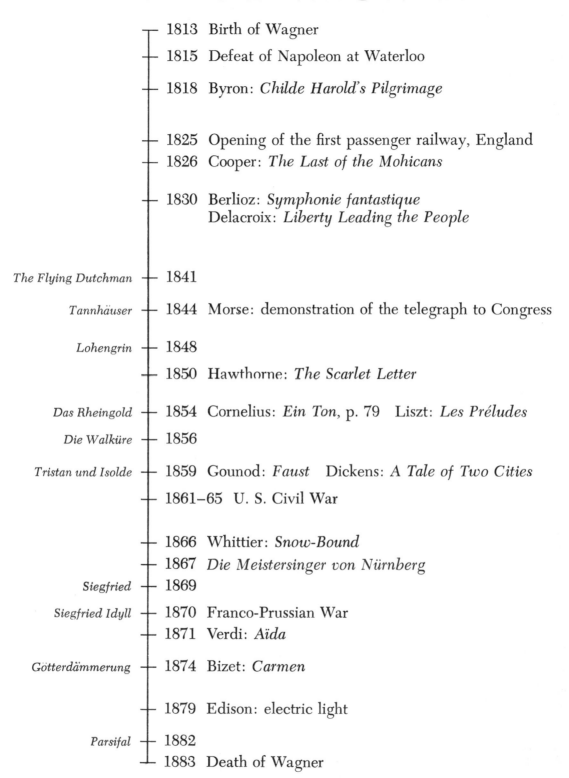

	1813	Birth of Wagner
	1815	Defeat of Napoleon at Waterloo
	1818	Byron: *Childe Harold's Pilgrimage*
	1825	Opening of the first passenger railway, England
	1826	Cooper: *The Last of the Mohicans*
	1830	Berlioz: *Symphonie fantastique* Delacroix: *Liberty Leading the People*
The Flying Dutchman	1841	
Tannhäuser	1844	Morse: demonstration of the telegraph to Congress
Lohengrin	1848	
	1850	Hawthorne: *The Scarlet Letter*
Das Rheingold	1854	Cornelius: *Ein Ton*, p. 79 Liszt: *Les Préludes*
Die Walküre	1856	
Tristan und Isolde	1859	Gounod: *Faust* Dickens: *A Tale of Two Cities*
	1861–65	U. S. Civil War
	1866	Whittier: *Snow-Bound*
	1867	*Die Meistersinger von Nürnberg*
Siegfried	1869	
Siegfried Idyll	1870	Franco-Prussian War
	1871	Verdi: *Aïda*
Götterdämmerung	1874	Bizet: *Carmen*
	1879	Edison: electric light
Parsifal	1882	
	1883	Death of Wagner

SCORED FOR LISTENING

Richard Wagner

Die Meistersinger von Nürnberg: Prelude

144

145

146

SCORED FOR SINGING

Richard Wagner
Die Meistersinger von Nürnberg: Prelude, Measures 76–89

JOHANNES BRAHMS

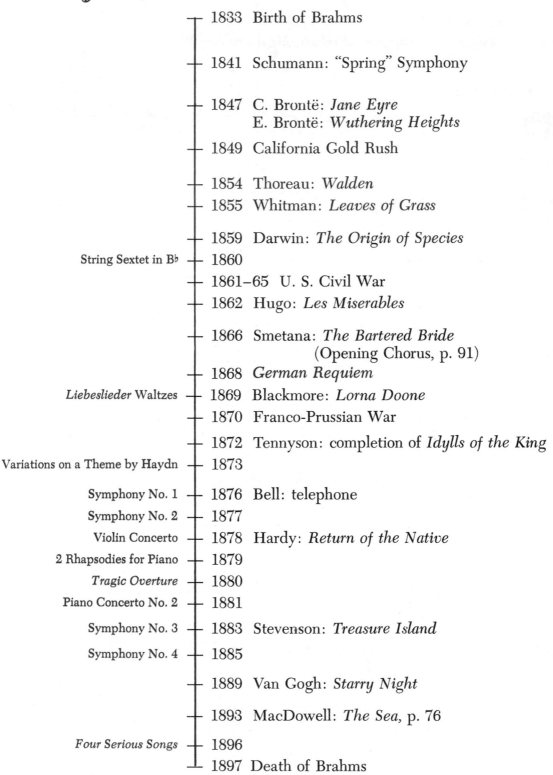

	1833	Birth of Brahms
	1841	Schumann: "Spring" Symphony
	1847	C. Brontë: *Jane Eyre* E. Brontë: *Wuthering Heights*
	1849	California Gold Rush
	1854	Thoreau: *Walden*
	1855	Whitman: *Leaves of Grass*
	1859	Darwin: *The Origin of Species*
String Sextet in B♭	1860	
	1861–65	U. S. Civil War
	1862	Hugo: *Les Miserables*
	1866	Smetana: *The Bartered Bride* (Opening Chorus, p. 91)
	1868	*German Requiem*
Liebeslieder Waltzes	1869	Blackmore: *Lorna Doone*
	1870	Franco-Prussian War
	1872	Tennyson: completion of *Idylls of the King*
Variations on a Theme by Haydn	1873	
Symphony No. 1	1876	Bell: telephone
Symphony No. 2	1877	
Violin Concerto	1878	Hardy: *Return of the Native*
2 Rhapsodies for Piano	1879	
Tragic Overture	1880	
Piano Concerto No. 2	1881	
Symphony No. 3	1883	Stevenson: *Treasure Island*
Symphony No. 4	1885	
	1889	Van Gogh: *Starry Night*
	1893	MacDowell: *The Sea*, p. 76
Four Serious Songs	1896	
	1897	Death of Brahms

SCORED FOR SINGING

Johannes Brahms

German Requiem: How Lovely Is Thy Dwelling Place

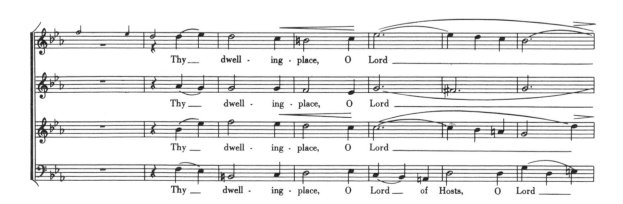

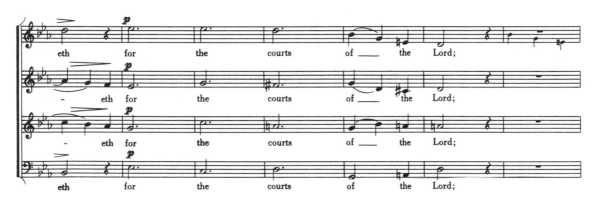

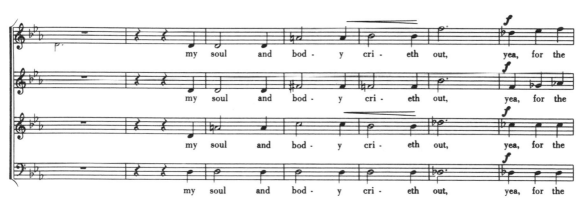

151

yea, for the liv - - - - - - - ing God.

yea, for the liv - ing, yea, for the liv - - - - - - ing God.

yea, for the liv - - - ing, yea, for the liv - - - ing God.

yea, for the liv - - - ing, yea, for the liv - ing God.

How love - ly, is Thy

How love - ly is Thy

How love - ly is Thy

How love - ly is Thy

dwell - ing - place, O Lord of Hosts, O Lord of Hosts,

dwell - ing - place, O Lord of Hosts, O Lord of Hosts,

dwell - ing - place, O Lord of Hosts, O Lord of Hosts,

dwell - ing - place, O Lord, O Lord of Hosts, O Lord of Hosts,

Thy dwell - ing - place, O Lord

Thy dwell - ing - place, O Lord

Thy dwell - ing - place, O Lord

Thy dwell - ing - place, O Lord of Hosts, O

MODEST MUSSORGSKY

1839 Birth of Mussorgsky

1841 Emerson: *Essays*

1842 Chopin: Polonaise in A♭

1845 Poe: "The Raven"

1846 Mendelssohn: *Elijah*

1848 Marx & Engels: *Communist Manifesto*

1851 Melville: *Moby-Dick*

1852 Stowe: *Uncle Tom's Cabin*

1854 Crimean War

1855 Longfellow: *Song of Hiawatha*

1857 Flaubert: *Madame Bovary*

1858 Saint-Saëns: *Christmas Oratorio*
    ("Praise Ye the Lord of Hosts," p. 82)

1861 Emancipation of the Russian serfs
1861–65 U. S. Civil War

Savishna (Love Song of the Idiot) — 1865 Whistler: *Old Battersea Bridge*

1866 Tolstoy: *War and Peace*
    Dostoievsky: *Crime and Punishment*

A Night on the Bare Mountain — 1867

1868 Grieg: Piano Concerto in A minor

Boris Godunov (1st version) — 1869

1870 Franco-Prussian War

1871 Mendeleyev: Periodic Law (properties of elements)

Boris Godunov (2nd version) — 1872

1874 *Pictures at an Exhibition*

Songs and Dances of Death — 1875–77

1877 Tchaikovsky: *Swan Lake*

1881 Death of Mussorgsky

SCORED FOR LISTENING

Mussorgsky-Ravel
Pictures at an Exhibition (Excerpts)

Promenade

Gnomus

158

Promenade

Tuileries (Children at Play)

Promenade

Ballet of Chicks in Their Shells

160

The Great Gate of Kiev

161

SCORED FOR SINGING

Modest Mussorgsky
Pictures at an Exhibition: Promenade, Measures 1 – 4
The Great Gate of Kiev, Measures 30 – 46

Promenade, Measures 1 – 4

The Great Gate of Kiev, Measures 30 – 46

CLAUDE DEBUSSY

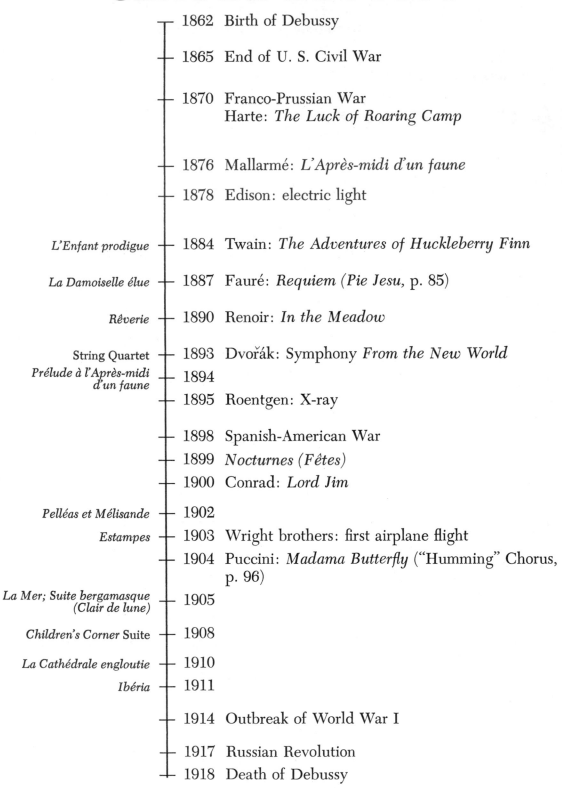

	1862	Birth of Debussy
	1865	End of U. S. Civil War
	1870	Franco-Prussian War Harte: *The Luck of Roaring Camp*
	1876	Mallarmé: *L'Après-midi d'un faune*
	1878	Edison: electric light
L'Enfant prodigue	1884	Twain: *The Adventures of Huckleberry Finn*
La Damoiselle élue	1887	Fauré: *Requiem (Pie Jesu,* p. 85)
Rêverie	1890	Renoir: *In the Meadow*
String Quartet	1893	Dvořák: Symphony *From the New World*
Prélude à l'Après-midi d'un faune	1894	
	1895	Roentgen: X-ray
	1898	Spanish-American War
	1899	*Nocturnes (Fêtes)*
	1900	Conrad: *Lord Jim*
Pelléas et Mélisande	1902	
Estampes	1903	Wright brothers: first airplane flight
	1904	Puccini: *Madama Butterfly* ("Humming" Chorus, p. 96)
La Mer; Suite bergamasque (Clair de lune)	1905	
Children's Corner Suite	1908	
La Cathédrale engloutie	1910	
Ibéria	1911	
	1914	Outbreak of World War I
	1917	Russian Revolution
	1918	Death of Debussy

164

SCORED FOR LISTENING

Claude Debussy
Nocturnes: Fêtes

169

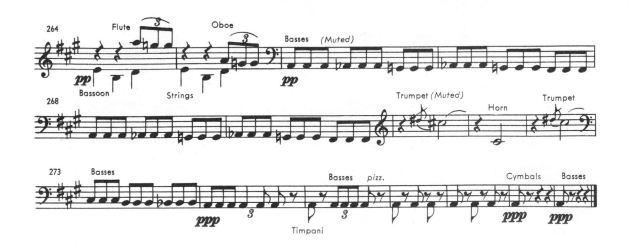

SCORED FOR SINGING

Claude Debussy
Nocturnes: Fêtes, Measures 98–109 and 120–139

Measures 98–109

MAURICE RAVEL

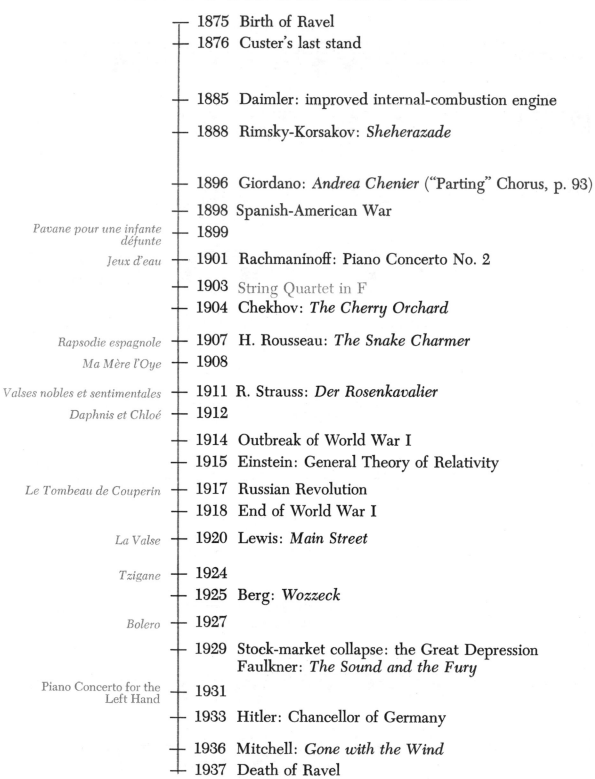

	1875	Birth of Ravel
	1876	Custer's last stand
	1885	Daimler: improved internal-combustion engine
	1888	Rimsky-Korsakov: *Sheherazade*
	1896	Giordano: *Andrea Chenier* ("Parting" Chorus, p. 93)
	1898	Spanish-American War
Pavane pour une infante défunte	1899	
Jeux d'eau	1901	Rachmaninoff: Piano Concerto No. 2
	1903	String Quartet in F
	1904	Chekhov: *The Cherry Orchard*
Rapsodie espagnole	1907	H. Rousseau: *The Snake Charmer*
Ma Mère l'Oye	1908	
Valses nobles et sentimentales	1911	R. Strauss: *Der Rosenkavalier*
Daphnis et Chloé	1912	
	1914	Outbreak of World War I
	1915	Einstein: General Theory of Relativity
Le Tombeau de Couperin	1917	Russian Revolution
	1918	End of World War I
La Valse	1920	Lewis: *Main Street*
Tzigane	1924	
	1925	Berg: *Wozzeck*
Bolero	1927	
	1929	Stock-market collapse: the Great Depression Faulkner: *The Sound and the Fury*
Piano Concerto for the Left Hand	1931	
	1933	Hitler: Chancellor of Germany
	1936	Mitchell: *Gone with the Wind*
	1937	Death of Ravel

Maurice Ravel
String Quartet in F: Movement 2

174

SCORED FOR SINGING

Maurice Ravel
String Quartet in F: Movement 2, Measures 1 – 11 and 162 – 169

Measures 1 – 11

Measures 162 – 169

IGOR STRAVINSKY

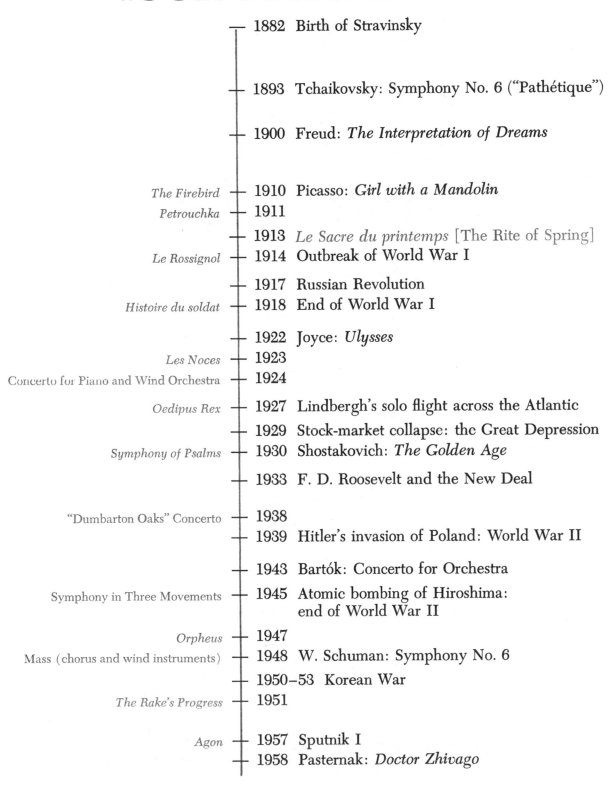

	1882	Birth of Stravinsky
	1893	Tchaikovsky: Symphony No. 6 ("Pathétique")
	1900	Freud: *The Interpretation of Dreams*
The Firebird	1910	Picasso: *Girl with a Mandolin*
Petrouchka	1911	
	1913	*Le Sacre du printemps* [The Rite of Spring]
Le Rossignol	1914	Outbreak of World War I
	1917	Russian Revolution
Histoire du soldat	1918	End of World War I
	1922	Joyce: *Ulysses*
Les Noces	1923	
Concerto for Piano and Wind Orchestra	1924	
Oedipus Rex	1927	Lindbergh's solo flight across the Atlantic
	1929	Stock-market collapse: the Great Depression
Symphony of Psalms	1930	Shostakovich: *The Golden Age*
	1933	F. D. Roosevelt and the New Deal
"Dumbarton Oaks" Concerto	1938	
	1939	Hitler's invasion of Poland: World War II
	1943	Bartók: Concerto for Orchestra
Symphony in Three Movements	1945	Atomic bombing of Hiroshima: end of World War II
Orpheus	1947	
Mass (chorus and wind instruments)	1948	W. Schuman: Symphony No. 6
	1950–53	Korean War
The Rake's Progress	1951	
Agon	1957	Sputnik I
	1958	Pasternak: *Doctor Zhivago*

SCORED FOR LISTENING

Igor Stravinsky

The Rite of Spring: Introduction, Dance of the Youths and Maidens

Introduction

Dance of the Youths and Maidens

181

Igor Stravinsky
The Rite of Spring: Dance of the Youths and Maidens, Measures 1 – 8 and 119 – 130

Measures 1 – 8 (Rhythm pattern)

Chant on a neutral syllable or clap

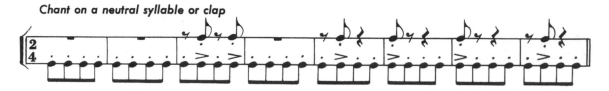

Measures 119 – 130

SERGEI PROKOFIEV

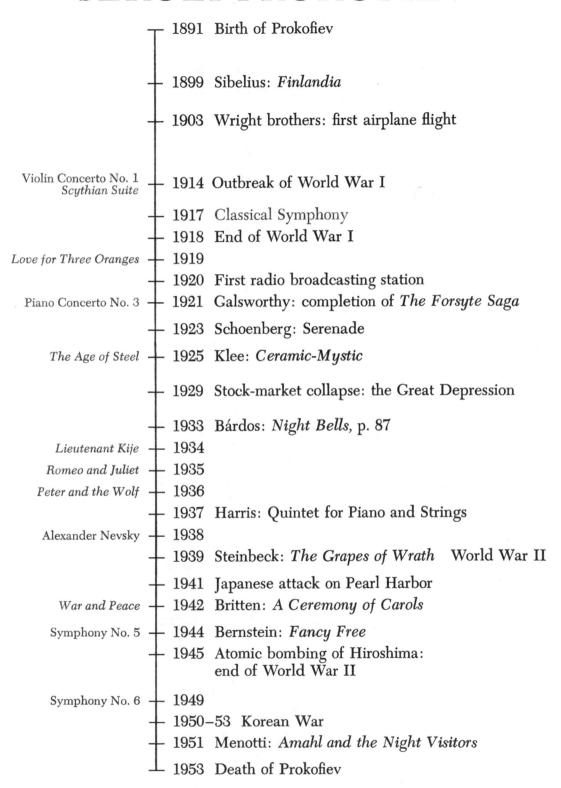

	1891	Birth of Prokofiev
	1899	Sibelius: *Finlandia*
	1903	Wright brothers: first airplane flight
Violin Concerto No. 1 *Scythian Suite*	1914	Outbreak of World War I
	1917	Classical Symphony
	1918	End of World War I
Love for Three Oranges	1919	
	1920	First radio broadcasting station
Piano Concerto No. 3	1921	Galsworthy: completion of *The Forsyte Saga*
	1923	Schoenberg: Serenade
The Age of Steel	1925	Klee: *Ceramic-Mystic*
	1929	Stock-market collapse: the Great Depression
	1933	Bárdos: *Night Bells*, p. 87
Lieutenant Kije	1934	
Romeo and Juliet	1935	
Peter and the Wolf	1936	
	1937	Harris: Quintet for Piano and Strings
Alexander Nevsky	1938	
	1939	Steinbeck: *The Grapes of Wrath* World War II
	1941	Japanese attack on Pearl Harbor
War and Peace	1942	Britten: *A Ceremony of Carols*
Symphony No. 5	1944	Bernstein: *Fancy Free*
	1945	Atomic bombing of Hiroshima: end of World War II
Symphony No. 6	1949	
	1950–53	Korean War
	1951	Menotti: *Amahl and the Night Visitors*
	1953	Death of Prokofiev

SCORED FOR LISTENING

Sergei Prokofiev

Classical Symphony

Movement 1

184

185

186

Movement 2

187

Movement 3 Gavotte

Movement 4 Finale

SCORED FOR SINGING

Sergei Prokofiev
Classical Symphony: Movement 2, Measures 5–12

GEORGE GERSHWIN

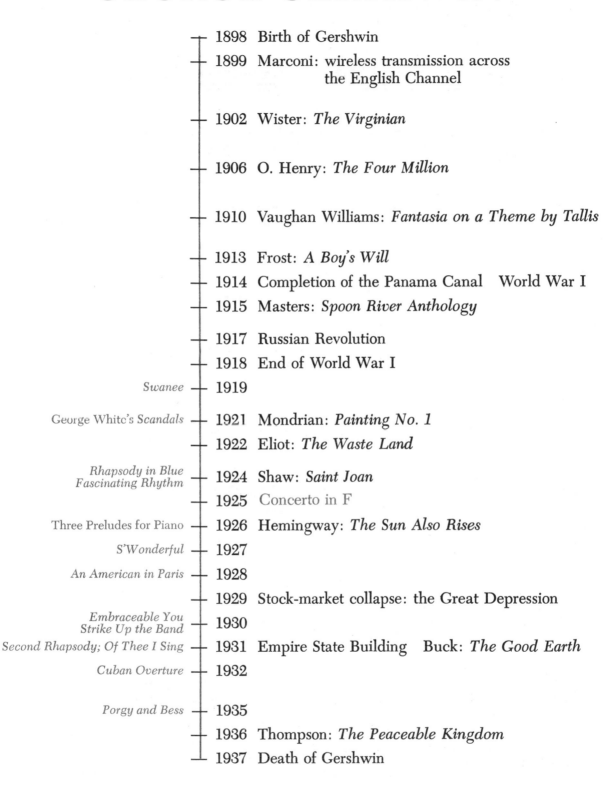

	1898	Birth of Gershwin
	1899	Marconi: wireless transmission across the English Channel
	1902	Wister: *The Virginian*
	1906	O. Henry: *The Four Million*
	1910	Vaughan Williams: *Fantasia on a Theme by Tallis*
	1913	Frost: *A Boy's Will*
	1914	Completion of the Panama Canal World War I
	1915	Masters: *Spoon River Anthology*
	1917	Russian Revolution
	1918	End of World War I
Swanee	1919	
George White's Scandals	1921	Mondrian: *Painting No. 1*
	1922	Eliot: *The Waste Land*
Rhapsody in Blue *Fascinating Rhythm*	1924	Shaw: *Saint Joan*
	1925	Concerto in F
Three Preludes for Piano	1926	Hemingway: *The Sun Also Rises*
S'Wonderful	1927	
An American in Paris	1928	
	1929	Stock-market collapse: the Great Depression
Embraceable You *Strike Up the Band*	1930	
Second Rhapsody; Of Thee I Sing	1931	Empire State Building Buck: *The Good Earth*
Cuban Overture	1932	
Porgy and Bess	1935	
	1936	Thompson: *The Peaceable Kingdom*
	1937	Death of Gershwin

SCORED FOR LISTENING

George Gershwin
Concerto in F: Movement 3 (Themes)

194

AARON COPLAND

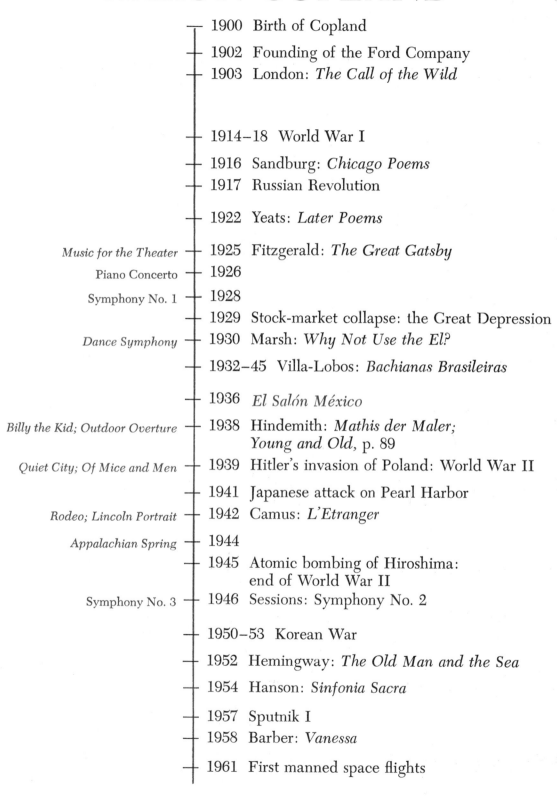

	1900	Birth of Copland
	1902	Founding of the Ford Company
	1903	London: *The Call of the Wild*
	1914–18	World War I
	1916	Sandburg: *Chicago Poems*
	1917	Russian Revolution
	1922	Yeats: *Later Poems*
Music for the Theater	1925	Fitzgerald: *The Great Gatsby*
Piano Concerto	1926	
Symphony No. 1	1928	
	1929	Stock-market collapse: the Great Depression
Dance Symphony	1930	Marsh: *Why Not Use the El?*
	1932–45	Villa-Lobos: *Bachianas Brasileiras*
	1936	*El Salón México*
Billy the Kid; Outdoor Overture	1938	Hindemith: *Mathis der Maler; Young and Old*, p. 89
Quiet City; Of Mice and Men	1939	Hitler's invasion of Poland: World War II
	1941	Japanese attack on Pearl Harbor
Rodeo; Lincoln Portrait	1942	Camus: *L'Etranger*
Appalachian Spring	1944	
	1945	Atomic bombing of Hiroshima: end of World War II
Symphony No. 3	1946	Sessions: Symphony No. 2
	1950–53	Korean War
	1952	Hemingway: *The Old Man and the Sea*
	1954	Hanson: *Sinfonia Sacra*
	1957	Sputnik I
	1958	Barber: *Vanessa*
	1961	First manned space flights

SCORED FOR LISTENING

Aaron Copland
El Salón México

197

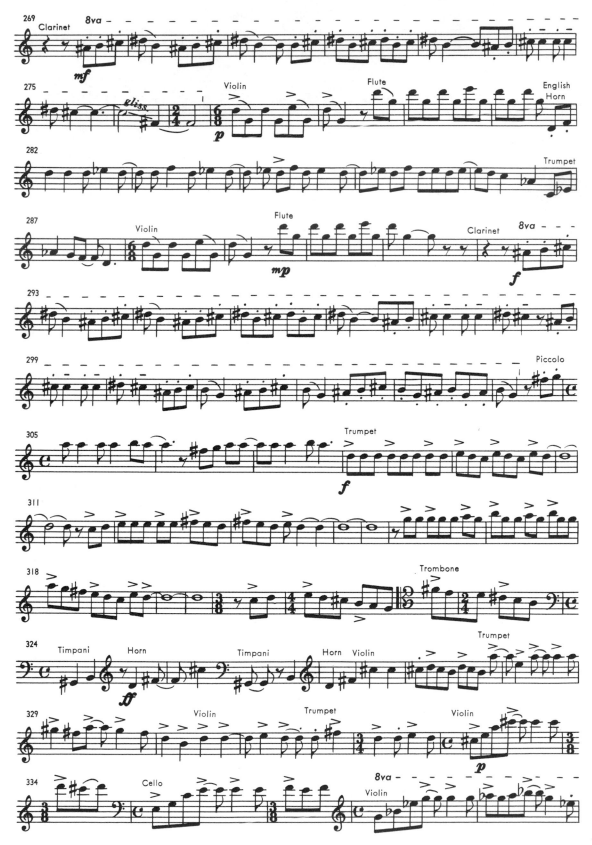

Twelve Famous Composers

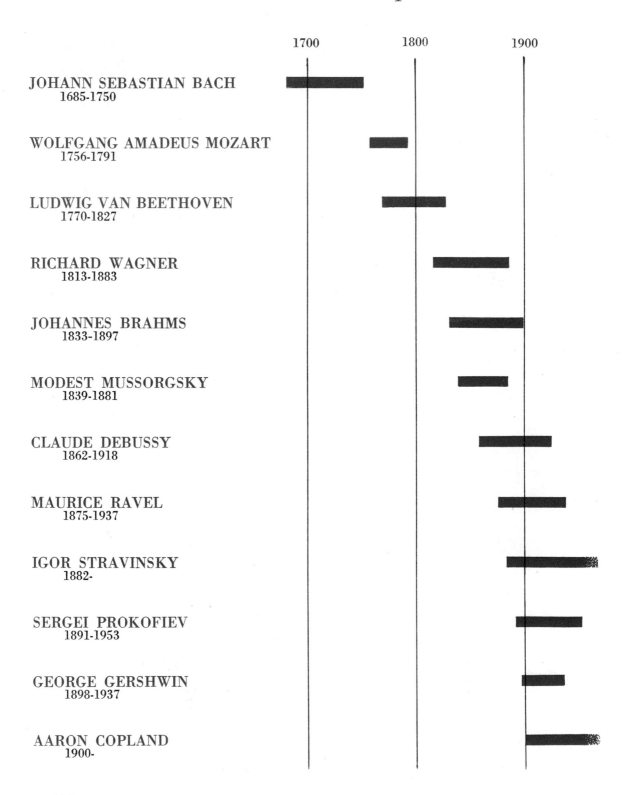

1700   1800   1900

JOHANN SEBASTIAN BACH
1685-1750

WOLFGANG AMADEUS MOZART
1756-1791

LUDWIG VAN BEETHOVEN
1770-1827

RICHARD WAGNER
1813-1883

JOHANNES BRAHMS
1833-1897

MODEST MUSSORGSKY
1839-1881

CLAUDE DEBUSSY
1862-1918

MAURICE RAVEL
1875-1937

IGOR STRAVINSKY
1882-

SERGEI PROKOFIEV
1891-1953

GEORGE GERSHWIN
1898-1937

AARON COPLAND
1900-

Letters and Opinions

LITERATURE ABOUT MUSIC is almost as old as music itself. Many libraries offer a wide range of books about music. These books include personal letters and memoirs of famous composers, the opinions of music critics, and scholarly research that explores every aspect of music and music history. The letters and opinions that follow will acquaint you with this kind of literature. You will discover that these documents touch on a variety of topics, such as musical style, the attitude of the public toward music in a given era, and the evaluation of a composer and his work by his contemporaries and later historians. Some of these documents are written in a matter-of-fact, humorous, or satirical style. You will grasp the idea of these writers at once. To understand others fully, you will want to consult a dictionary or encyclopedia.

All of the documents in this book have been selected because they say something specific. You will find them thought-provoking, and they should lead to interesting discussions about the music in our heritage — and music today.

JOHANN SEBASTIAN BACH

A Contract to Perform

We, the sworn Burgomasters of Muehlhausen, Free City of the Holy Empire, and Members of the Council of the Parish of St. Blasius', herewith make known that, as the post of organist there is open, having become vacant through the decease of our late friend and colleague, Mr. Johan Georg Ahle, we have called hither, in order to fill the said post, Mr. Johann Sebastian Bach of the Third Church at Arnstadt, and have engaged him as our organist in the said Church of St. Blasius, on the conditions that he be loyal and true above all to the Magistrate of this town, not alone defend our common city from all harm but also work for its best interests, show himself willing in the execution of the duties required of him and be available at all times, particularly attend to his service faithfully and industriously on Sundays, Feast Days, and other Holy Days, keep the organ entrusted to him at least in good condition, call the attention of those serving at any time as the appointed supervisors to any defects found in it and industriously watch over its repairs and *music*, be zealous in observing all the requirements of a decent and respectable life, also avoid unseemly society and suspicious *compagnie;* and just as the said Mr. Bach has obligated himself by a handshake to show his agreement with all the foregoing and to conduct himself accordingly, so we have promised to give him, as his yearly salary:

85 gulden in money and the following emoluments in kind:

54 bushels of grain,

2 cords of wood, 1 beech and 1 oak or aspen,

6 times threescore fagots delivered to the door instead of acreage,

and having accordingly had the present certificate of appointment executed, with the seal of the Chancellery affixed.

(L.S.) Parishioners of Muehlhausen
Imperial Free City of the Holy Empire.
Done the 15th of June, 1707.

The Bach Reader, Hans T. David and Arthur Mendel, eds. New York: W. W. Norton & Company, Inc., 1945, p. 55.

Music and Architecture

. . . we may apply to Bach's organ works in general a term that has been given to architecture, and say that they are "construction beautified." By this is meant that every feature, however beautiful in itself, finds its final charm and justification only as a necessary component in the comprehensive plan. . . . In their superb rolling harmonies . . . their long-drawn cadences, and their thrilling climaxes, they seem to possess a fit relation to the vaulted, reverberating ceilings, the massive pillars, and the half-lighted recesses of the sombre old buildings in which they had their birth.

Music in the History of the Western Church, Edward Dickinson. New York: Charles Scribner's Sons, 1903, p. 293.

Viewpoint on Style

Leonard Bernstein: . . . we are used to hearing a melody on top, with chords supporting it underneath like pillars – melody and harmony, a tune and its accompaniment. . . . That's our basic idea of music, only because in the last two hundred years or so music has grown in that direction.

But before that, people used to listen to music differently. The ear was conditioned to hear *lines*, simultaneous melodic lines, rather than chords. That was the natural way of music, strange though it seems to us. Counterpoint came before harmony, which is a comparatively recent phenomenon. Actually, all primitive music, like Oriental folk music today, is made of *lines*, just as present-day jazz is also primarily involved with line. That's why jazzmen idolize Bach. For them, he is the great model for the continuously running melody, and this is natural, because Bach and the jazz player both feel music in terms of line – that is, horizontally.

* * * * *

What I hope you're beginning to see is that harmony and counterpoint are interactive, and that there is something of each involved in the other. I have been warned that this is too subtle a point for the nonmusician to grasp, but I don't believe it. And this point is most exciting, because it is the key to Bach's style. Bach fuses the vertical and the horizontal in so marvelous a way that you can never say of any piece of his, "This is only counterpoint," or "This is only harmony." He fashions a kind of sublime crossword puzzle in which the notes of the across "words" and the down "words" are interdependent, where everything checks and all the answers are right.

The Joy of Music, Leonard Bernstein. New York: Simon and Schuster, 1959, pp. 233 and 236.

Reverent Respect

Berlioz: When one comes from Paris and knows our musical customs, one must witness the respect, the attention, the piety with which a German audience listens to such a composition [*St. Matthew Passion*], to believe it. Every one follows the words of the text with his eyes; not a movement in the house, not a murmur of approbation or blame, not the least applause; they are listening to a sermon, hearing the Gospel sung; they are attending in silence, not a concert but a divine service. And it is really thus that this music ought to be listened to. They adore Bach, and believe in him, without supposing for an instant that his divinity can ever be questioned; a heretic would horrify them; it is even forbidden to speak on the subject. Bach is Bach, as God is God.

The Composer as Listener, Irving Kolodin, ed. New York: Horizon Press, 1958, pp. 20–21.

Music for Some People

Mendelssohn, in a letter to Zelter, Munich, June 22, 1830: The organist [in Weimar] offered me the choice of hearing something scholarly, or something for "people" (because he said that, for people in general, one must compose only easy and bad music), so I asked him for something scholarly. But it was not much to be proud of; he modulated around enough to make one giddy, but nothing unusual came of it; he made a number of entries, but no fugue was forthcoming. When my turn came to play to him, I started with the D minor toccata of Sebastian and remarked that this was at the same time scholarly and something for "people" too, at least for some of them; but mind, hardly had I begun to play when the superintendent dispatched his valet upstairs with the message that this playing had to be stopped right away because it was a weekday and he could not study with that much noise going on. . . .

Felix Mendelssohn Letters, G. Selden-Goth, ed. New York: Pantheon Books Inc., 1945, pp. 81–82.

— *But not the Critics*

Charles Burney, 1789: If Sebastian Bach and his admirable son Emanuel, instead of being musical-directors in commercial cities, had been fortunately employed to compose for the stage and public of great capitals, such as Naples, Paris, or London, and for performers of the first class, they would doubtless have simplified their style more to the level of their judges . . . and both, by writing in a style more popular, and generally intelligible and pleasing, would have extended their fame, and been indisputably the greatest musicians of the present century.

A General History of Music, Charles Burney, 1789. Frank Mercer, ed. New York: Dover Publications, Inc., 1957. Vol. II, p. 955.

Johann Adolph Scheibe, in *Der Critische Musikus*, Hamburg, May 14, 1737: This great man would be admired by the whole nation, had he more agreeableness and did he not keep naturalness away from his compositions by employing bombastic and intricate devices and darkening beauty with overelaborate art. He judges the difficulties of his music according to his fingers. His compositions, therefore, are difficult to perform, as he demands that singers and instrumentalists perform with their throats and instruments the same feats he can perform on the clavier. This, of course, is impossible. All the ornaments, all the little grace notes, and all that are known as *agréments* are written out in full. Therefore his compositions are deprived of beauty, of harmony, and of clarity of melody, since the song is unrecognizable. All voices must work with each other, all with the same weight, so that it is impossible to recognize the principal voice.

Composer and Critic, Max Graf. New York: W. W. Norton & Company, Inc., 1946, p. 80.

Twentieth-Century Appraisal

Vaughan Williams, in a lecture, 1932: One of the three great composers of the world (personally I believe the greatest) was Johann Sebastian Bach. Here, you may say, is the universal musician if ever there was one; yet no one could be more local, in his origin, his life work, and his fame for nearly a hundred years after his death, than Bach. He was to outward appearance no more than one of a fraternity of town organists and "town pipers" whose business it was to provide the necessary music for the great occasions in church and city. He never left his native country, seldom even his own city of Leipzig. "World movements" in art were then unheard of; moreover, it was the tradition of his own country which inspired him. True, he studied eagerly all the music of foreign composers that came his way in order to improve his craft. But is not the work of Bach built up on two great foundations, the organ music of his Teutonic predecessors and the popular hymn tunes of his own people?

National Music, Ralph Vaughan Williams. New York: Oxford University Press, 1934, p. 5.

WOLFGANG AMADEUS MOZART

Music for the Public

The eighteenth century marks the emergence of the middle class as an influential segment of society. As this increasingly wealthy bourgeois class pressed for recognition within a world dominated by the aristocracy, it strove to assimilate the culture and ideals of the court. Taste and learning no longer remained the exclusive property of the nobility but were ever more widely disseminated among the members of the middle class. . . . Their demands for increased participation in the musical life formerly confined almost entirely to courtly circles led to the establishment of new musical institutions. Informal associations of amateurs banded together to perform music for their own edification and amusement. But the primary means by which the musical appetite of this large new audience could be satisfied became the public concert. With this new institution came many of the features of musical life that still exist today. To fill the ample spaces of public halls with sound, larger ensembles of instruments were called for and the symphony orchestra was evolved. The newly invented pianoforte with its greater volume of sound soon replaced the harpsichord and clavichord. The touring virtuoso came upon the scene to dazzle and bewitch his listeners with his incredible technique. As a result new categories of composition appeared and old ones, unsuited to contemporary tastes, disappeared.

The Art of Music, Beekman C. Cannon, Alvin H. Johnson, William G. Waite. New York: Thomas Y. Crowell Company, 1960, pp. 294–295.

Mozart at the Age of Nine

Friedrich Melchior Grimm, in his "Correspondence littéraire," 1764: And this curious boy is now nine years old. He has grown hardly at all, but he has made wonderful progress in music. As early as two years ago he has composed and edited sonatas; and since then, he has had six sonatas printed for the Queen of England; six for the Princess of Nassau-Weilburg; he has composed Symphonies for a large orchestra, that have been performed and were acclaimed with great praise. He has even written several Italian arias, and I am not giving up hope, that he will have written an opera for some Italian theatre before he is twelve years old. He heard Manzuoli in London all winter long, and has made such good use of this, that he, although his voice is very small, sings with both feeling and taste. But the most unbelievable of all is his profound knowledge of harmony and its intricate ways, so that the Prince of Brunswick, truest judge in these matters, has said that many a superior Kapellmeister would die without ever having learned what this nine year old boy already knows. We have seen him for an hour and a half under the impact storm of musicians from whose brows the perspiration ran down in streams, and who had all the trouble in the world, to withdraw, creditably, from this struggle with a boy who left the battle field without the least sign of fatigue. I have seen him confuse and bring to silence organists who considered themselves most proficient.

The Book of Musical Documents, Paul Nettl, ed. New York: Philosophical Library, Inc., 1948, p. 147.

A Musical Joke

Mozart possessed a healthy sense of humor. One of his compositions, named *A Musical Joke*, was intended to ridicule inexpert village bands. In it, there is a violin cadenza containing a whole-tone scale; there are parallel fifths in defiance of all established rules. As a climax, the piece ends in several different keys.

Nowadays, these harmonies are no longer funny. The whole-tone scale is part and parcel of French impressionism. Parallel fifths are used by composers writing in the neoclassical idiom. And the simultaneous playing of different keys has acquired the scientific name of polytonality. Mozart, of course, could not in his wildest dreams have imagined that his innocent pranks would a century and a half later become the serious practice of important composers.

A Thing or Two About Music, Nicolas Slonimsky, ed. New York: Allen, Towne & Heath, Inc., 1948, p. 93.

The Mozart Music

Tchaikovsky, in his diary, 1886: According to my deep conviction, Mozart is the highest, the culminating point that *beauty* has attained in the sphere of music. No one has made me weep, has made me tremble with rapture, from the consciousness of my nearness to *that something* which we call the *ideal*, as he has done.

The Diaries of Tchaikovsky, Wladimir Lakond, ed. and tr. New York: W. W. Norton & Company, Inc., 1945, p. 248.

Aaron Copland: There is no way to *seize* the Mozart music. This is true even for a fellow-composer, any composer, who, being a composer, rightfully feels a special sense of kinship, even a happy familiarity, with the hero of Salzburg. After all, we can pore over him, dissect him, marvel or carp at him. But in the end there remains something that will not be *seized*. That is why, each time a Mozart work begins — I am thinking of the finest examples now — we composers listen with a certain awe and wonder, not unmixed with despair. The wonder we share with everyone; the despair comes from the realization that only this one man at this one moment in musical history could have created works that seem so effortless and so close to perfection.

Copland on Music, Aaron Copland. Garden City: Doubleday & Company, Inc., 1960, pp. 105–106.

Bernard Shaw, in *The World*, London, April 19, 1893: In the ardent regions where all the rest are excited and vehement, Mozart alone is completely self-possessed: where they are clutching their bars with a grip of iron and forging them with Cyclopean blows, his gentleness of touch never deserts him: he is considerate, economical, practical under the same pressure of inspiration that throws your Titan into convulsions.

. . . The true Parnassian air acts on these people like oxygen on a mouse: it first excites them, and then kills them. Give me the artist who breathes it like a native, and goes about his work in it as quietly as a common man goes about his ordinary business. Mozart did so; and that is why I like him. Even if I did not, I should pretend to; for a taste for his music is a mark of caste among musicians, and should be worn, like a tall hat, by the amateur who wishes to pass for a true Brahmin.

Music in London 1890–94, Bernard Shaw. London: Constable and Company, Ltd., 1932. Vol. II, pp. 286–287.

The Universal Language?

The attractions of Mozart's music for a universal audience are seldom admitted. The finish and perfection of his music are supposed to be attractive only to relatively sophisticated audiences. In this connection it is worth noting that a recent explorer among the Indians in territory between Venezuela and Brazil found that a Mozart Symphony played on a portable phonograph was an *open sesame* to them. The Indians were indifferent to Sousa's *Stars and Stripes Forever* and to Louis Armstrong, but they were mad about Mozart.

An Introduction to Music, David D. Boyden. New York: Alfred A. Knopf, Inc., 1956, p. 280.

LUDWIG VAN BEETHOVEN

New Sounds for a New Era

At the turn of the century and at the same time that the French Revolution was committing the old structure of feudal society to the flames, Beethoven began to transform the symphonic forms he had inherited from Haydn. He enlarged the framework of the symphony with the composition of the *Eroica*. He had a new feeling for greatness and for masses of sound. He clothed symphonic forms in a dramatic atmosphere. The delicate, chamber-music style of the symphony, which had originated in the candle-lit rooms of palaces, gave way to a new abundance of chords, to music that no longer chattered but spoke in the thunder tones of a mighty speech. Broad, arching planes appeared in his work, and mighty chords struck the ears of his auditors. Passionate feelings were tossed up as the sea tosses up waves in a storm. Dynamics were charged with explosive energy, as if man had become once more an elemental being, passionate and wild; like Prometheus, defying the heavens and quarreling with Jove himself. Within the music we find also new poetical forces: symphonic music had become the language of humanity, for now were heard funeral marches and fantastic scherzos with Shakespearian overtones, as well as prayers and hymns whose solemnity had never before been equaled.

Composer and Critic, Max Graf. New York: W. W. Norton & Company, Inc., 1946, pp. 147–148.

The Man

From Beethoven's Notebooks and Calendars, 1812: Resignation, the most sincere resignation to your fate! Only this can make you capable of the sacrifices which your duty and vocation demand. O hard struggle! Do everything in your power to make all the necessary arrangements for your distant journey. You must find all those things that guarantee the realization of your most treasured wish; thus, in spite of it all, you must win through by defiance, be absolutely true to your constant conviction.

You must not be human, not for yourself, only for others: for you there can be no more happiness, except within yourself, in your art. Oh, God! give me strength to conquer myself! For nothing must bind me to this life.

Beethoven, Letters, Journals and Conversations, Michael Hamburger, ed. and tr. New York: Pantheon Books Inc., 1952, p. 121.

The Creative Process

Into the notebooks he had begun to keep before he was out of his teens, he now began to crowd that welter of musical ideas, in all stages of development, which make the notebooks comparable to Leonardo's. To examine them is to be vouchsafed a unique opportunity to see the unfolding — hesitant, baffled, and inspired — of genius. Starting with what may seem an unpromising, even banal, sequence of notes, adding to them, subtracting, emphasizing, finally perfecting, Beethoven worked — sometimes for decades — at these viable fragments. Many a composition which seems like the product of a single mighty inspiration was pieced together from these apparently unrelated sketches. In a very real sense, it may be said that from the very beginning of his creative life, Beethoven was at work on all of his compositions.

Men of Music, Wallace Brockway and Herbert Weinstock. New York: Simon and Schuster, Inc., 1958, pp. 168–169.

Beethoven, from a written conversation with Louis Schlösser, 1822 or 1823: I carry my thoughts about with me for a long time, often for a very long time, before writing them down. I can rely on my memory for this and can be sure that, once I have grasped a theme, I shall not forget it even years later. I change many things, discard others, and try again and again until I am satisfied; then, in my head, I begin to elaborate the work in its breadth, its narrowness, its height, its depth and, since I am aware of what I want to do, the underlying idea never deserts me. It rises, it grows, I hear and see the image in front of me from every angle, as if it had been cast [like sculpture], and only the labor of writing it down remains, a labor which need not take long, but varies according to the time at my disposal, since I very often work on several things at the same time. Yet I can always be sure that I shall not confuse one with another. You may ask me where I obtain my ideas. I cannot answer this with any certainty: they come unbidden, spontaneously or unspontaneously. I may grasp them with my hands in the open air, while walking in the woods, in the stillness of night, at early morning. Stimulated by those moods which poets turn into words, I turn my ideas into tones which resound, roar and rage until at last they stand before me in the form of notes.

Beethoven, Letters, Journals and Conversations, Michael Hamburger, ed. and tr. New York: Pantheon Books Inc., 1952, pp. 194–195.

The Struggle

From the autobiography of Louis Spohr: As, at the time when I made his acquaintance, Beethoven had ceased to perform either in public or at private gatherings, I was only given a single opportunity of hearing him, when by chance I went to see him during the rehearsal of a new trio (D major, triple time). It was hardly an enjoyable experience; for, to begin with, the piano was badly out of tune, a circumstance which troubled Beethoven little as, in any case, he could not hear the music, and secondly scarcely anything remained of the artist's once so greatly admired virtuosity, also because of his deafness. In the *forte* passages the poor deaf man struck the instrument with such violence that the strings rattled, while in the *piano* passages he played so softly that whole bars were inaudible and the music became unintelligible if one was unable to follow the pianoforte part in manuscript. I was overpowered by a feeling of deep sorrow when I considered this hard fate. If it is a great misfortune for anyone to be deaf, how can a musician endure it without despairing? Beethoven's chronic melancholia no longer puzzled me.

Beethoven, Letters, Journals and Conversations, Michael Hamburger, ed. and tr. New York: Pantheon Books Inc., 1952, pp. 110–111.

Precision in Tempo

Beethoven, in a letter to Ignaz von Mosel, Vienna, 1817: I am delighted to know that you share my opinion of those headings, inherited from times of musical barbarism, by which we describe the tempo of a movement. What, for example, can be more absurd than 'allegro' which, once and for all, means 'cheerful'? How far removed we often are from this meaning! . . . We would do well to dispense with headings. The words which describe the character of the piece are a very different matter. These we could not give up; whereas the tempo is really no more than the body, these refer rather to the spirit of the piece. I have often thought of giving up these absurd terms allegro, andante, adagio, presto. Mälzel's metronome gives us an excellent opportunity to do so. I give you my word, in my future compositions I shall not use them.

Beethoven, Letters, Journals and Conversations, Michael Hamburger, ed. and tr. New York: Pantheon Books Inc., 1952, p. 161.

Objection

The Harmonicon, London, July 1825: The merits of Beethoven's Seventh Symphony we have before discussed, and we repeat, that . . . it is a composition in which the author has indulged a great deal of disagreeable eccentricity. Often as we now have heard it performed, we cannot yet discover any design in it, neither can we trace any connection in its parts. Altogether, it seems to have been intended as a kind of enigma—we had almost said a hoax.

Lexicon of Musical Invective, Nicolas Slonimsky, ed. New York: Coleman-Ross Company, Inc., 1953, p. 44.

Objection Overruled

During his lifetime he was acclaimed the foremost composer of his age; at his death all Vienna mourned, and twenty thousand people watched his funeral procession; he became the universal genius of music, and his work was placed on such a pinnacle that it became the standard by which every note of music written after him had ultimately to be judged. Not only an adoring public but the greatest masters of music who followed him—Schubert, Schumann, Wagner, Brahms—freely acknowledged his sovereignty. There have been periods in the past when Beethoven's music seemed destined for a decline, the inevitable result of overpraise and overplaying; but as yet the various recessions have never proceeded very far. Even today, after his works and his life together have passed under the devastating X-rays of modern criticism, his eminence in music is but partly challenged. Only one other name has so far entered the lists to dispute Beethoven's priority, and it is not the name of a follower but of a predecessor—Johann Sebastian Bach.

The Stream of Music, Richard Anthony Leonard. Garden City: Doubleday, Doran & Company, Inc., 1943, p. 88.

RICHARD WAGNER

The Magic of the Stage

Wagner: What particularly attracted me to the theater—by which I mean the stage itself, the rooms behind the scenes, and the dressing rooms—was not so much the desire for entertainment and distraction, as it is with the theatrical public of the present day, but the provocative delight of being in an element that opposed to the impressions of everyday life an absolutely different world, one that was purely fantastic, and with a touch of horror in its spell. Thus to me a stage setting, even a wing representing merely a bush, or a costume, or even a characteristic part of one, seemed to have come from another world, to have a sort of ghostly interest, and I felt that the contact with it must be a lever to lift me from the commonplace reality of the routine of daily life to that enchanting demon world.

Music in History, Howard D. McKinney and W. R. Anderson. New York: American Book Company, 3rd edition, 1957, pp. 631–632.

A Super-Art

What he wanted to do was to make a powerful dramatic story, clothed in the splendor of poetry, the real object of his endeavor, with the music simply one of the hand-maidens which would point up and intensify that drama. To accomplish this would require a radically new approach to the various elements of opera. A new type of poetry would have to be written, a special kind of drama, and an entirely different kind of music. All the old stylized forms and practices—the set numbers, the arias, the choruses, the old divisions into scenes, etc.—would have to be thrown out of the window; instead the music would have to flow along continually with the drama in order to give it the movement of reality.

The Stream of Music, Richard Anthony Leonard. Garden City: Doubleday, Doran & Company, Inc., 1943, p. 225.

Wagner's Orchestra

Technically, Wagner was an opera composer, and his main reforms, as he thought of them, were carried out in the realm of dramatic music. Actually, he was one of the century's great masters of orchestral writing, whose innovations in harmony and instrumentation, as well as intensity of emotional pitch, exerted incalculable influence on the whole domain of Romantic music. Indeed, it is hardly an exaggeration to say that Wagner's music shaped the entire course of orchestral writing in the second half of the century. . . . In any case, Wagnerism represents the very culmination of Romanticism, a brilliant, impassioned style of overwhelming – sometimes almost brutal – power, of dazzling orchestral color and virtuosity, so distinctive that some historians of the nineteenth-century art use it as a landmark.

Listening to Music Creatively, Edwin John Stringham. Englewood Cliffs, N. J.: Prentice-Hall, Inc., 2nd edition, 1959, p. 335.

The focal point of Wagnerian music drama . . . is . . . the orchestra. Here is the nub of his operatic reform. He had inherited the orchestral language and the symphonic art of Beethoven, and it became his mission to introduce these into the lyric theatre. In so doing he developed a type of symphonic opera as native to the German genius as vocal opera is to the Italian. The orchestra is the unifying principle of his music drama. It is both participant and ideal spectator; it remembers, prophesies, reveals, comments. The orchestra is fate and primal force, flooding the action, the characters, and the audience in a torrent of sound that incarnates the sensuous ideal of the romantic era: a sumptuous sound shot with color and light, which for sheer imaginativeness is unsurpassed in nineteenth-century art.

The Enjoyment of Music, Joseph Machlis. New York: W. W. Norton & Company, Inc., 1955, p. 225.

Die Meistersinger — Contrasting Views

John Ruskin, in a letter to Mrs. Burne-Jones, June 30, 1882: Of all the bête, clumsy, blundering, boggling, baboon-blooded stuff I ever saw on a human stage,

that thing last night *(Meistersinger)* beat – as far as the story and acting went; and of all the affected, sapless, soulless, beginningless, endless, topless, bottomless, topsy-turviest, tongs – and boniest doggerel of sounds I ever endured the deadliness of, that eternity of nothing was the deadliest – as far as the sound went.

Lexicon of Musical Invective, Nicolas Slonimsky, ed. New York: Coleman-Ross Company, Inc., 1953, p. 243.

Bernard Shaw, in *The Hawk*, London, August 13, 1889: I am a seasoned Wagnerian; and there is no veil of strangeness between me and the ocean of melody . . . in Die Meistersinger. . . . That third act, though conducted by Hans Richter, who is no sluggard, lasts two hours; and the strain on the attention, concentrated as it is by the peculiarities of the theatre, is enormous. . . . When it is over you are glad you went through with it, and are even willing to face it again; but you recognize that you have achieved edification by a great feat of endurance, and that your holiday, your enjoyment, your relaxation will come when the work of witnessing the performance is finished.

How to Become a Musical Critic, Bernard Shaw. Dan H. Laurence, ed. New York: Hill and Wang, 1961, p. 150.

The Dictator

Bernard Shaw, in *The Dramatic Review*, London, February 8, 1885: It is not easy to make an English orchestra nervous, but Wagner's tense neuralgic glare at the players as they waited for the beat with their bows poised above the strings was hard upon the sympathetic men, whilst the intolerable length of the pause exasperated the tougher spirits. When all were effectually disconcerted, the composer's *bâton* was suddenly jerked upwards, as if by a sharp twinge of gout in his elbow; and, after a moment of confusion, a scrambling start was made. During the performance Wagner's glare never relaxed: he never looked pleased. When he wanted more emphasis he stamped; when the division into bars was merely conventional he disdained counting, and looked daggers—spoke them too, sometimes—at innocent instrumentalists who were enjoying the last few bars of their rest without any suspicion that the impatient composer had just discounted half a stave or so and was angrily waiting for them. When he laid down the *bâton* it was with the air of a man who hoped he might never be condemned to listen to such a performance again.

How to Become a Musical Critic, Bernard Shaw. Dan H. Laurence, ed. New York: Hill and Wang, 1961, p. 52.

JOHANNES BRAHMS

A Composer from Hamburg

Schumann, in "Gesammelte Schiften [*sic*] ueber Musik und Musiker": He came from Hamburg, where he created in solitude and silence, initiated by an excellent, inspiring master into the most difficult fields of art. He bore all the insignia of one to be announced to us: "Behold one of the elect."

Sitting at the piano—and he has a marvelous style of playing—he opened to us wonderful new vistas, and we were drawn, more and more, into his magic circle. He made of the piano an orchestra of lamentation and exultation. There were sonatas, mostly symphonies in disguise; songs, the poetry of which could be understood without knowing the words, for a deep song melody pervades them; various pieces for the piano of sometimes demoniac character but charming in form; sonatas for violin and piano; quartets for string instruments, so diversified, that they seemed to spring from different sources. And were he to touch, with his wand, the mass power of orchestra and chorus, wonderful glimpses into a phantom world might await us.

The Book of Musical Documents, Paul Nettl, ed. New York: Philosophical Library, Inc., 1948, p. 237.

The German Requiem

His choral works culminate in the German Requiem, which will remain his most beloved work, a Protestant Office for the Dead such as German music had not known since the days of its great Biblical composers of the baroque era. Unlike the Latin Requiem Mass which prepares the souls for the *Dies Irae*, this German Requiem comforts the bereaved, an unspeakable peace envelops the whole work, and only once, in the terrifying unison passages of the mysterious funeral march, are we reminded of the tragedy of death.

Music in Western Civilization, Paul Henry Lang. New York: W. W. Norton & Company, Inc., 1941, p. 903.

A Critical Composer

Tchaikovsky, in a letter to the Grand Duke Constantine, October 2 (14), 1888: In the music of this master . . . there is something dry and cold which repulses me. He has very little melodic invention. He never speaks out his musical ideas to the end. Scarcely do we hear an enjoyable melody, than it is engulfed in a whirlpool of unimportant harmonic progressions and modulations, as though the special aim of the composer was to be unintelligible. He excites and irritates our musical senses without wishing to satisfy them, and seems ashamed to speak the language which goes straight to the heart. . . . He has set before himself, once and for all, the aim of trying to be profound, but he has only attained to an appearance of profundity. . . . It is impossible to say that the music of Brahms is weak and insignificant. His style is invariably lofty. He does not strive after mere external effects. He is never trivial. All he does is serious and noble, but he lacks the chief thing – beauty. Brahms commands our respect. We must bow before the original purity of his aspirations. We must admire his firm and proud attitude in the face of triumphant Wagnerism; but to love him is impossible. I, at least, in spite of much effort, have not arrived at it.

The Life & Letters of Peter Ilich Tchaikovsky, Modeste Tchaikovsky. Rosa Newmarch, ed. (from the Russian). New York: John Lane Company, 1906, pp. 570–571.

Other Critics

Boston Traveler, **February 27, 1882:** It would appear as though Brahms might afford occasionally to put a little more melody into his work – just a little now and then for a change. His Second Symphony gave the impression that the composer was either endeavoring all the while to get as near as possible to harmonic sounds without reaching them; or that he was unable to find any whatever.

Lexicon of Musical Invective, Nicolas Slonimsky, ed. New York: Coleman-Ross Company, Inc., 1953, p. 70.

Bernard Shaw, in *The World*, London, December 23, 1891: Brahms has always had the mere brute force of his amazing musical faculty. No one can deny that he all but equals our most famous native orators in respect of having a power of utterance that would place him above the greatest masters if only he had anything particular to say.

How to Become a Musical Critic, Bernard Shaw. Dan H. Laurence, ed. New York: Hill and Wang, 1961, p. 201.

Brahms Speaks of Himself

Letter to Koessler, 1894: I have gone far: I am respected both by my friends and my opponents. Even though I am not loved by all, – I am respected, and that is the main thing. I ask for no more. I know very well what my position in the history of music is going to be: the position that Cherubini had, and still has today. That is my lot, my fate. . . .

The Book of Musical Documents, Paul Nettl, ed. New York: Philosophical Library, Inc., 1948, p. 260.

A Historical View

Technically speaking, he invented nothing; he changed nothing. His preoccupation with what had gone before him and his disdain of trends toward the future were so fundamental that many of his contemporaries . . . failed to recognize him as a romantic composer at all. In certain respects he was like Bach, who, in summing up the age of polyphony at its close, was left a lonely and monastic figure, his work old-fashioned in a world which had moved on toward newer standards.

Brahms's music might easily have suffered the neglect that Bach's did. What saved it was the institution of the public concert, by his time well established in Western society, and the rise of the commercial publisher — two factors which served to keep his work steadily before the public eye. . . . His was the best-loved and best-hated music of the nineteenth century. As late as 1900, Philip Hale in Boston could say, "This way out in case of Brahms," and still retain the vestments of his critical reputation. Only during the past few decades has Brahms reached the ultimate heights; he is now a box-office attraction.

The Stream of Music, Richard Anthony Leonard. Garden City: Doubleday, Doran & Company, Inc., 1943, pp. 253–254.

MODEST MUSSORGSKY

A Musical Art Exhibit

Pictures at an Exhibition by Moussorgsky* is an interesting instance of a composition that has made its mark both in the original piano version and in orchestral investitures by Ravel and others. The work can also claim distinction on the grounds that it is one of the few in the repertory that has successfully incorporated the visual arts as the basis of a poetic programme. . . . The exhibit referred to in the title was a memorial showing of sketches, architectural drawings, and water-colors by the composer's friend Victor Hartmann, which was held in St. Petersburg (now Leningrad) in 1874 shortly after the artist's death. These drawings, most of which are now lost, are by no means to be reckoned among the imperishable masterpieces of art. They do reveal, however, that Russian architects such as Hartmann were searching for national sources of Russian art, just as Moussorgsky and his colleagues were looking for national idioms in musical expression. The coincidence of their ideas happily resulted in the present work.

Understanding Music, William Fleming and Abraham Veinus. New York: Henry Holt and Company, 1958, pp. 224–225.

Musical Barbarian or Gentleman?

Tchaikovsky, in a letter to von Meck, December 1878: With regard to Moussorgsky, as you very justly remark, he is 'used up.' His gifts are perhaps the most remarkable of all, but his nature is narrow and he has no aspirations towards self-perfection. He has been too easily led away by the absurd theories of his set and the belief in his own genius. Besides which his nature is not of the finest quality, and he likes what is coarse, unpolished, and ugly. He is the exact opposite of the distinguished and elegant Cui.

Moussorgsky plays with his lack of polish — and even seems proud of his want of skill, writing just as it comes to him, believing blindly in the infallibility of his genius. As a matter of fact his very original talent flashes forth now and again.

The Critical Composer, Irving Kolodin, ed. New York: Howell, Soskin & Co., 1940, pp. 200–201.

Debussy: He will leave an indelible impression on the minds of those who love him or who will love him in time to come. No one has given utterance to the best within

*Variations exist in the spelling of names transliterated from a language (such as Russian) that does not have a Latin alphabet.

215

us in tones more gentle and profound; he is unique and will remain so because his art is spontaneous and free from arid formulas. Never has a more refined sensibility been conveyed by such simple means; it is like the art of an inquiring savage, discovering music step by step through his emotions.

Composer and Critic, Max Graf. New York: W. W. Norton & Company, Inc., 1946, p. 290.

Without Honor

Rimsky-Korsakov: Mussorgsky's music is published and performed only in my arrangements, without which it could not possibly be placed on a concert program or published. Since Mussorgsky's days we have made some progress. To compose like Mussorgsky nowadays is disgraceful.

A Thing or Two About Music, Nicolas Slonimsky. New York: Allen, Towne & Heath, Inc., 1948, p. 156.

The Test of Time

He was so little understood that after his death his best friend, Rimsky-Korsakov, tried to cover up what seemed to be Mussorgsky's musical ignorance. Rimsky-Korsakov edited many of the works for publication, "touching them up to make them more understandable to the public," ironing out the "technical mistakes." This well-meant act of a devoted friend had in the long run a totally different effect than anyone had foreseen. A new generation arose years afterward which found the originals far more inspired than the painted-over substitutions. The Mussorgsky who had been belittled as a bungler became one of the dynamos of twentieth-century music, with ideas and technique enough to galvanize some of the best musical minds of the present era.

The Stream of Music, Richard Anthony Leonard. Garden City: Doubleday, Doran & Company, Inc., 1943, p. 291.

CLAUDE DEBUSSY

"I Like It that Way!"

Debussy, one of the most instinctive musicians who ever lived, was the first composer of our time who dared to make his ear the sole judge of what was good harmonically. With Debussy, analysts found chords that could no longer be explained according to the old harmony. If one had asked Debussy why he used such chords, I am sure he would have given the only possible answer: "I like it that way!"

What to Listen for in Music, Aaron Copland. New York: McGraw-Hill Book Company, Inc., 1957, p. 73.

Pictures in Sound

. . . impressionist music wavered between major and minor without adhering to either. In this way was abandoned one of the basic contrasts of classical harmony. Impressionism advanced the disintegration of the major-minor system. It floated in a borderland between keys, creating elusive effects that might be compared to the misty outlines of impressionist painting.

These evanescent harmonies demanded colors no less subtle. No room here for the thunderous climaxes of the romantic orchestra. Instead there was a veiled blending of hues, an impalpable shimmer of pictorial quality: flutes and clarinets in their dark lower register, violins in their lustrous upper range, trumpets and horns discreetly muted; and over the whole a silvery gossamer of harp, celesta, and triangle; glockenspiel, muffled drum, and cymbal brushed with a drumstick.

The Enjoyment of Music, Joseph Machlis. New York: W. W. Norton & Company, Inc., 1955, p. 483.

A New Language

Debussy's impressionism was far more than merely a personal style. It also included an immense new technical apparatus which gave the composers who came after him a whole new set of tools with which to work. This fact is only recently being realized — now that Debussy's ideas have permeated musical thought the world over. His uses of neglected scales like the whole-tone and pentatonic scales, his revival of the medieval modes and organum, his bold use of totally unrelated chords, his reliance upon chords of the seventh, ninth, eleventh, and thirteenth — above all his treatment of the chord as an element of beauty apart from melody — all these ideas can now be found in imitation in the music of every country, in popular mediums like music for sound films, and even in the commonest dance-band arrangements. They are part of the new language of music.

The Stream of Music, Richard Anthony Leonard. Garden City: Doubleday, Doran & Company, Inc., 1943, p. 364.

The Color of a Chord

. . . the science of harmony is concerned largely with the progression of chords, and

. . . its rules govern principally the passage from one chord to another. Debussy looked upon a chord as a color medium which could be entirely independent of anything that came before it or followed it. Thus dissonance became an end in itself, and not merely a temporary disturbance of the ear which must be set at rest by a consonance. When Debussy wrote dissonant chords he had little thought of resolving them, for his chords were entities which he could arrange in any way his taste dictated.

This Modern Music, John Tasker Howard. New York: Thomas Y. Crowell Company, 1942, p. 80.

Nocturnes

Debussy's account of his Nocturnes for orchestra shows how instinctively he tended to express himself as a painter. . . . The title, Nocturnes, he explained, was "*not meant to designate the usual form of the nocturne,*" but was intended in the sense of "the variety of impressions and the special effects of light that the word suggests." By careful exclusion, neither its literal meaning as a night piece, nor its common musical meaning in romantic piano music (for instance, the Chopin Nocturnes) as an indrawn mood piece is intended. The notion that the word *nocturne* suggests "special effects of light" obviously is derived not from music, but from painting.

Understanding Music, William Fleming and Abraham Veinus. New York: Henry Holt and Company, 1958, p. 384.

Fêtes

"Fêtes" is a crowded, phantasmagoric canvas of brilliant effect; at the same time it is light as air, impalpable and visionary as the dream stuff of the mind. An exotic rhythmic structure, complex and wayward, animates the whole work. The melodies fly past like themes blown along the wind; at the close they are like tunes heard at a distance in the hot languor of the summer night – vague, unfinished, vanishing into air at the touch. The pageant which interrupts this "argent revelry" is one of those breathless moments of sheer effect which has no equal in impressionistic music: distant trumpets and throbbing harps announce the coming of some new cavalcade of maskers; within the space of a few bars the orchestral scene is suddenly ablaze with magic light and color – and then in an instant they have all vanished, their themes calling back from afar as the whole scene fades away.

The Stream of Music, Richard Anthony Leonard. Garden City: Doubleday, Doran & Company, Inc., 1943, p. 355.

MAURICE RAVEL

The Sound of Chamber Music

The most usual chamber-music combinations in use at the present time are the trio, the quartet, and the quintet, and some of the world's greatest music has been written for these combinations. In hearing such a group play, the amateur is almost always disappointed after having become familiar with one of the great orchestral works. And there is reason for his disappointment; his natural mistake is in confusing volume with quality of tone. He is disappointed perhaps that he is listening to only three or four instruments instead of a hundred; he misses the overpowering magnitude and splendid weight of the orchestral mass; there is no flashing contrast of colors, no surge of composite tone, no tremendous contrast in dynamics. The very picture before his eyes is disappointing; instead of a large group of instrumentalists, each of them blending his personality and activity with a hundred others under the kindling fire and burning enthusiasm of the conductor, he sees only three, four, or five players huddled in the middle of the stage, each of them closely engaged in reading his own music without the magnetic stimulus of a visible leader. Everything seems cool, calculated, cerebral.

But let him listen for other things! The clear sonority of the various instruments as they blend together or answer one another in dialogue or repartee; the strength of the whole, due to the equal importance of each part; the weighty matters upon which the instruments discourse – all these are worth his careful attention.

Discovering Music. Howard D. McKinney and W. R. Anderson. New York: American Book Company, 4th edition, 1962, p. 193.

Quartet in F — A Triumph

Ravel's Quartet, the first of his masterpieces, was written when he was only twenty-eight. It is one of his most spontaneous works. Many years later, at the height of his mastery, Ravel regarded this youthful work with satisfaction; he said that though his later chamber music revealed greater technical adroitness, he preferred the Quartet for its freshness.

The Quartet, which Ravel dedicated to Fauré, was Ravel's first major success. Introduced by the Heyman Quartet on March 5, 1904, at a concert of the Société Nationale in Paris, it was a triumph. Some critics did not hesitate to call it a masterpiece. "In the name of the gods of music and of my own," Debussy wrote to the young composer, "do not change one thing in your Quartet!"

The Complete Book of 20th Century Music, David Ewen. Englewood Cliffs, N. J.: Prentice-Hall, Inc., 1959, pp. 312–313.

— But not in New York

New York Tribune, December 12, 1906: In his String Quartet, M. Ravel is content with one theme which has the emotional potency of one of those tunes which the curious may hear in a Chinese theater, shrieked out by an ear-splitting clarinet. This theme serves him for four movements during which there is about as much emotional nuance as warms a problem in algebra. It is a drastic dose of wormwood and assafoetida.

Lexicon of Musical Invective, Nicolas Slonimsky, ed. New York: Coleman-Ross Company, Inc., 1953, p. 138.

Debussy and Ravel

There is an enameled brightness about Ravel's music that contrasts with the twilight softness of Debussy's. He is less visionary. His rhythms are more incisive and have a verve, a drive that Debussy rarely strives for. His mind is more precise, his humor dryer, his harmonies crisper. He goes beyond Debussy's conception of dissonance. He is more conventional in respect to form, and his melodies are broader in span, more direct. His texture is contrapuntal, often being based on the interplay of lines rather than on the vertical blocks of sound that fascinated Debussy. . . . Whereas Debussy aimed to "decongest" sound, treating each instrument as a soloist, Ravel handled the huge post-romantic orchestra with brilliant virtuosity, and with special emphasis on what has well been called the confectionary department - harp glissandos, glockenspiel, celesta, triangle.

The Enjoyment of Music, Joseph Machlis. New York: W. W. Norton & Company, Inc., 1955, pp. 493–494.

IGOR STRAVINSKY

A Turning Point

When the future historians of the twentieth century, taking the long view of its happenings, decide upon its pivotal events and circumstances, they will find May 29, 1913, a date to be reckoned with. In the field of modern music it will hold a place as crucial as the political and military crisis that shook the world fourteen months later.

On that evening at the Théâtre des Champs Elysées, in Paris, Sergei Diaghilev produced a new ballet, "Le Sacre du printemps [The Rite of Spring]." The choreography, as performed by Diaghilev's famous Russian dancers, was by Nijinsky, with scenery and costumes by Nicholas Roerich. Igor Stravinsky composed the music.

The Parisians who attended that première performance could not have come with the intention of creating a fiasco even more scandalous than the one provided half a century before by Wagner's *Tannhäuser,* but they succeeded nevertheless in doing just that. What enraged them and turned them into two warring factions, yelling, hissing, and stamping in defiance, was the music —a score of such cacophonous fury and emotional violence that it struck many listeners with the force of an explosion.

The Stream of Music, Richard Anthony Leonard. Garden City: Doubleday, Doran & Company, Inc., 1943, p. 387.

A Violent Audience

A certain part of the audience, thrilled by what it considered to be a blasphemous attempt to destroy music as an art, and swept away with wrath, began very soon after the rise of the curtain to whistle, to make cat-calls, and to offer audible suggestions as to how the performance should proceed. Others of us, who liked the music and felt that the principles of free speech were at stake, bellowed defiance. It was war over art for the rest of the evening and the orchestra played on unheard, except occasionally when a slight lull occurred. The figures on the stage danced in time to music they had to imagine they heard and beautifully out of rhythm with the uproar in the auditorium. I was sitting in a box in which I had rented one seat. Three ladies sat in front of me and a young man occupied the place behind me. He stood up during the course of the ballet to enable himself to see more clearly. The intense excitement under which he was laboring, thanks to the potent force of the music, betrayed itself presently when he began to beat rhythmically on the top of my head with his fists. My emotion was so great that I did not feel the blows for some time. They were perfectly synchronized with the beat of the music. When I did, I turned around. His apology was sincere. We had both been carried beyond ourselves.

Music after the Great War, Carl Van Vechten. New York: G. Schirmer, Inc., 1915, pp. 87–88.

Music's New Dimensions

More than any other single composition, it has influenced composers throughout the world, setting forth a new trend in musical composition, helping to evolve a new idiom. The dynamism of Stravinsky's rhythmic writing—the rapidly changing meters, the counterpoint of different rhythms—had a devastating kinesthetic appeal; the tension of the music, built up through dissonance and polytonality, had a terrifying effect; the brazen colors produced by unorthodox instrumentation were dazzling; the primitive appeal to the elementary senses of masses of sound and disjointed melodies had overwhelming impact. All this destroyed the complacency not only of a first-night audience but also of an entire musical era.

The Complete Book of 20th Century Music, David Ewen. Englewood Cliffs, N. J.: Prentice-Hall, Inc., 1959, p. 406.

The Score

The orchestration, first of all, is masterly — a tour de force which has not been surpassed in three decades of orchestral writing. . . . His score is full of straining horns, trumpets, and trombones, shrill woodwinds, piccolos shrieking in the highest register, violent glissandos in the brass choir, percussion that shakes the very earth. Most of these effects were calculated to shock, but they were nevertheless powerfully evocative of the scene to be painted.

The score also contains some of Stravinsky's best melodic ideas. Most of his themes, although original, have the contours of crude folk tunes. They are sharp-pointed, pungent, purposely avoiding any hint of sensuous smoothness. All of them have the identity and the staying power which is the mysterious quality of all good melody. They cling to the mind long after the music has ceased. In the entire score there is hardly a measure of orthodox harmony. Dissonance and polytonality abound, with effects of deliberate harshness that set the teeth of the conservatives on edge. Moreover, there is no gliding over these dissonances by the use of soft strings. As often as not they are roared out with the full force of the brass.

The most extraordinary feature of "Le Sacre du printemps" remains Stravinsky's use of rhythm. He set a new standard of rhythmic complexity, with cadences sometimes so involved that the time signature changes with almost every bar – 3/8, 2/4, 3/4, 4/4, 5/4, 6/8, 7/8, etc. The piece abounds in furious energy of a type usually associated with expressions of the primitive emotions, the wild stampings and threshings of zealots, medicine men, and dervishes. Rhythm rises to such paramount importance in this work that it could be said Stravinsky uses it as Debussy did the chord – as an entity in itself, overshadowing melody in importance in the general scheme.

The Stream of Music, Richard Anthony Leonard. Garden City: Doubleday, Doran & Company, Inc., 1943, pp. 398–399.

Is Music a Language?

Stravinsky defines music as communication through sound. This generalization is sharply qualified by the distinction he makes between communication and self-expression. "Music," he writes, "is, by its very nature, essentially powerless to express anything at all, whether a feeling, an attitude of mind, a psychological mood, a phenomenon of nature. . . . Expression has never been an inherent property of music. If music appears to express something this is only an illusion and not a reality. It is simply an additional attribute which, unconsciously, only by force of habit we have come to confuse with its essential being."

If music is not essentially the communication of expressive feelings, what then does it communicate? Order, says Stravinsky. . . . Its indispensable and single requirement is construction. Construction once completed, this order has been attained; and "it is precisely this achieved order," he concludes, "which produces in us a unique emotion having nothing in common with our ordinary sensations and our responses to the feelings and impressions of daily life."

The Art of Music, Beekman C. Cannon, Alvin H. Johnson, and William G. Waite. New York: Thomas Y. Crowell Company, 1960, pp. 441–442.

SERGEI PROKOFIEV

"New" Melody

Prokofiev: Every now and then somebody or other starts urging me to put more feeling, more emotion, more melody in my music. My own conviction is that there is plenty of all that in it. I have never shunned the expression of feeling and have always been intent on creating melody – but new melody, which perhaps certain listeners do not recognize as such simply because it does not resemble closely enough the kind of melody to which they are accustomed.

The Concert Companion, Robert Bagar and Louis Biancolli. New York: McGraw-Hill Book Company, Inc., 1947, p. 526.

Contemporary but Pleasing

Prokofiev is one of the most successful of modern composers. He manages to write in contemporary style without unduly disturbing the public, which is very much on its guard against experimental composers. The reason for Prokofiev's popularity is probably that his music is surprisingly tuneful and has a humor and gaiety which are very attractive. Unlike some twentieth-century composers, his humor is not in distortion or in the use of conscious banality, but is inherent in his musical style, which is entirely spontaneous. There is a certain kinship with the musical wit of Haydn, as found in the finales to his symphonies. Prokofiev's music is festive and good natured, and a good antidote to the stern intellectuality of some contemporary music.

From Madrigal to Modern Music, Douglas Moore. New York: W. W. Norton & Company, Inc., 1942, p. 290.

Classical Symphony

This delightful symphony is a twentieth-century adaptation of the classical symphony of Mozart and Haydn. The form and instrumentation are of classical proportions; classical, too, are the economy and transparency of the orchestral writing and the brevity of the developments. But the harmonic progressions, the angular melodic lines with their capricious octave leaps, and the Prokofievian whimsy belong to our times. The strange blend of the past and the present, however, offers no contradiction. With all his customary mastery, Prokofiev has admirably synchronized old styles and new to create a living artistic product. This music is so simple and direct in its approach, so precise in the presenta-

tion of its thematic materials, and so terse and logical in its development that it can readily be assimilated at first hearing; and for these reasons it has been one of the most popular of Prokofiev's works.

The Complete Book of 20th Century Music, David Ewen. Englewood Cliffs, N. J.: Prentice-Hall, Inc., 1959, p. 285.

Ugly or Strong?

His clean muscular music, bubbling over with wit and whimsy, struck a fresh note. "I love melody," he declared, "and I regard it as the most important element in music. One must be especially careful to make sure that the melody retains its simplicity without becoming cheap, saccharine, or imitative. It is easy to say but not so easy to do." Beyond dispute he managed to do it. Characteristic are his athletic march rhythms, the harmonies pungently dissonant but rooted in the key, the sudden modulations, the unexpected turns of phrase, and the orchestral color that manifests all the brilliance we associate with the Russian school.

The Enjoyment of Music, Joseph Machlis. New York: W. W. Norton & Company, Inc., 1955, p. 560.

The Listener Must Judge

Musical America, New York, December 21, 1918: In these days when peace is heralded and the world is turning from dissonance to harmony, it comes as a shock to listen to such a program. Those who do not believe that genius is evident in superabundance of noise looked in vain for a new musical message in Mr. Prokofiev's work. Nor in the *Classical Symphony*, which the composer conducted, was there any cessation from the orgy of discordant sounds.

As an exposition of the unhappy state of chaos from which Russia suffers, Mr. Prokofiev's music is interesting, but one hopes fervently that the future may hold better things both for Russia and listeners to Russian music.

Lexicon of Musical Invective, Nicolas Slonimsky, ed. New York: Coleman-Ross Company, Inc., 1953, p. 133.

GEORGE GERSHWIN

Jazz — and a Master Composer

Gershwin: Jazz I regard as an American folk-music; not the only one, but a very powerful one which is probably in the blood and feeling of the American people more than any other style of folk-music. I believe that it can be made the basis of serious symphonic works of lasting value, in the hands of a composer with talent for both jazz and symphonic music.

American Composers on American Music, Henry Cowell, ed. Stanford, Calif.: Stanford University Press, 1933, p. 187.

Gershwin: It is difficult to determine what enduring values, aesthetically, jazz has contributed, because "jazz" is a word which has been used for at least five or six different types of music. It is really a conglomeration of many things. It has a little bit of ragtime, the blues, classicism and spirituals. Basically, it is a matter of rhythm. After rhythm, in importance come intervals, music intervals which are peculiar to the rhythm. After all, there is nothing new in music. I maintained years ago that there is very little difference in the music of different nations. There is just that little individual touch. One country may prefer a peculiar rhythm or a note like the seventh. This it stresses, and it becomes identified with that nation. In America this preferred rhythm is called jazz. Jazz is music; it uses the same notes that Bach used. When jazz is played in another nation, it is called American. When it is played in another country, it sounds false. Jazz is the result of the energy stored up in America. It is a very energetic kind of music, noisy, boisterous and even vulgar. One thing is certain. Jazz has contributed an enduring value to America in the sense that it has expressed ourselves. It is an original American achievement which will endure, not as jazz perhaps, but which will leave its mark on future music in one form or another. The only kinds of music which endure are those which possess form in the universal sense and folk-music. All else dies. But unquestionably folk-songs are being written and have been written which contain enduring elements of jazz. To be sure, that is only an element; it is not the whole. An entire composition written in jazz could not live.

Revolt in the Arts, Oliver M. Sayler. New York: Brentano's, 1930, pp. 266–267.

Concerto in F

Dr. Walter Damrosch, speaking at the première, December 3, 1925: Various composers have been walking around jazz like a cat around a plate of hot soup, waiting for it to cool off, so that they could enjoy it without burning their tongues, hitherto accustomed only to the more tepid liquid distilled by cooks of the classical school. Lady Jazz, adorned with her intriguing rhythms, has danced her way around the world, even as far as the Eskimos of the North and the Polynesians of the South Sea Isles. But for all her travels and her sweeping popularity, she has encountered no knight who could lift her to a level that would enable her to be received as a respectable member of the musical circles.

George Gershwin seems to have accomplished this miracle. He has done it boldly by dressing this extremely independent and up-to-date young lady in the classic garb of a concerto. Yet he has not detracted one whit from her fascinating personality. He is the Prince who has taken Cinderella by the hand and openly proclaimed her a princess to the astonished world, no doubt to the fury of her envious sisters.

The Concert Companion, Robert Bagar and Louis Biancolli. New York: McGraw-Hill Book Company, Inc., 1947, pp. 276–277.

John Tasker Howard was of the opinion that Gershwin's attempt to be formally correct in the Concerto "took away much of the natural charm that had been found in his previous *Rhapsody in Blue*." But a concerto for piano and orchestra is a work of art, not a work of nature, and the Concerto in F is a better work of art than the *Rhapsody in Blue*. When the English conductor Albert Coates, in 1930, named Gershwin's Concerto in F as one of the best musical compositions of all time—and the only one by an American to figure on his list—he

displayed remarkable acumen as well as exceptional courage. Today, more than a quarter of a century after its première, Gershwin's Concerto is firmly entrenched as the first work in that form by an American composer to have entered the permanent repertoire of symphonic music.

America's Music, Gilbert Chase. New York: McGraw-Hill Book Company, Inc., 1955, p. 492.

Music that Endures

It is mainly since Gershwin's death that complete awareness of his musical importance has become almost universal. The little defects in his major works—those occasional awkward modulations, the strained transitions, the obscure instrumentation—no longer appear quite so important as they did several decades ago. What many did not realize then—and what they now know—is that the intrinsically vital qualities of Gershwin's works reduce these technical flaws to insignificance. The music is so alive, so freshly conceived, and put down on paper with such spontaneity and enthusiasm that its youthful spirit refuses to age. The capacity of this music to enchant and magnetize audiences remains as great today, even with familiarity, as it was yesterday, when it came upon us with the freshness of novelty.

The Complete Book of 20th Century Music, David Ewen. Englewood Cliffs, N. J.: Prentice-Hall, Inc., 1959, p. 134.

AARON COPLAND

Spokesman for Modern Music

Copland: . . . the art of music has been passing through a period of revolutionary change. Although this break with the past

began more than forty years ago, there are still some people who have not yet recovered from the shock. Music has been changing, but they have remained the same. Nevertheless, inwardly, they know that change in music, like change in all the arts, is inevitable. After all, why should I or any other composer living in a time like ours write music that reflects some other period? Isn't it natural for us to try to develop our own kind of music? In doing so, we are merely following the example of revolutionaries like Beethoven and Wagner. They too sought new expressive possibilities in music—and found them.

The fact is that the whole history of music is a history of continuous change. There never was a great composer who left music exactly as he found it. This is true of Bach and Mozart, just as it is true of Debussy and Stravinsky. We can only conclude, therefore, that the period of change through which music has recently passed was, contrary to what many people believe, an inevitable one—part of the great tradition of music throughout the ages.

At any rate, whether we like it or not, music today is radically different from what it was fifty years ago.

* * * * *

Modern music, in a word, is principally the expression in terms of an enriched musical language of a new spirit of objectivity, attuned to our own times. It is the music of the composer of today—in other words, *our* music.

Our New Music, Aaron Copland. New York: McGraw-Hill Book Company, Inc., 1941, pp. vii–viii and 5.

A New Public—and a Goal

Copland: During these years [1930–1935] I began to feel an increasing dissatisfaction with the relations of the music-loving public and the living composer. The old "special" public of the modern music concerts had fallen away, and the conventional concert public continued apathetic or indifferent to anything but the established classics. It seemed to me that we composers were in danger of working in a vacuum. Moreover, an entirely new public for music had grown up around the radio and phonograph. It made no sense to ignore them and to continue writing as if they did not exist. I felt that it was worth the effort to see if I couldn't say what I had to say in the simplest possible terms.

Our New Music, Aaron Copland. New York: McGraw-Hill Book Company, Inc., 1941, pp. 228–229.

A Goal Achieved

There has been no cheapening of style or artistic concession in this conscious effort to write music that can be appreciated by the many instead of the few. On the contrary, in his later works Copland has grown in artistic stature. His language has become personalized, his speech has acquired subtler emotional nuances. Two of his works—*Appalachian Spring* and the Third Symphony—were selected by the New York Music Critics Circle as the best new works produced by an American during the season in which they were introduced; and *Appalachian Spring*, in addition, was awarded the Pulitzer Prize in music. "Here is at last," as Arthur V. Berger wrote, "an American that we may place unapologetically beside the recognized figures of any other country."

The Complete Book of 20th Century Music, David Ewen. Englewood Cliffs, N. J.: Prentice-Hall, Inc., 1959, p. 64.

El Salón México

Copland: During my first visit to Mexico, in the fall of 1932, I conceived the idea of writing a piece based on Mexican themes.

I suppose there is nothing strange in such an idea. Any composer who goes outside his native land wants to return bearing musical souvenirs. In this case my musical souvenirs must have been very memorable, since it wasn't until 1933 that I began to assemble them into the form of an orchestral work.

From the very beginning the idea of writing a work based on popular Mexican melodies was connected in my mind with a popular dance hall in Mexico City called Salón México. No doubt I realized, even then, that it would be foolish for me to attempt to translate into musical sounds the more profound side of Mexico; the Mexico of the ancient civilization or the revolutionary Mexico of today. In order to do that one must really know a country. All that I could hope to do was to reflect the Mexico of the tourists, and that is why I thought of the Salón México. Because in that "hot spot" one felt, in a very natural and unaffected way, a close contact with the Mexican people. It wasn't the music I heard, but the spirit that I felt there, which attracted me. Something of that spirit is what I hope to have put into my music.

I followed no general rule in the use of the themes that I treated. Almost all of them come from the *Cancionero Mexicano* by Frances Toor, or from the erudite work of Ruben M. Campos, *El folk-lore y la Musica Mexicana*. To both authors I owe thanks. Probably the most direct quotation of a complete melody is that of *El Mosco* (No. 84 in the book by Campos), which is presented twice, immediately after the introductory measures (in which may be found fragments of *El Palo Verde* and *La Jesusita*).

The Concert Companion, Robert Bagar and Louis Biancolli. New York: McGraw-Hill Book Company, Inc., 1947, p. 195.

Musician of Our Time

Whatever may be the ultimate verdict regarding the intrinsic value of Copland's music, or the degree of attention that posterity may bestow upon his compositions, he remains historically important as a musician who by the diversity and effectiveness of his output, by his impressive impact on America's musical activity at many different points, by his versatility, his adventurousness, and his industry, has participated with extraordinary completeness in the musical events of the contemporary world, not only in the concert hall, the theater, and the classroom, but also in such typical twentieth-century media of mass communication as the radio and the motion picture. Whatever posterity may say, we can only reply: "He was a musician of our times." We may turn to his compositions as to a compendium of twentieth-century trends in American music.

America's Music, Gilbert Chase. New York: McGraw-Hill Book Company, Inc., 1955, pp. 501–502.

Mind and Heart

Copland: Music demands an alert mind of intellectual capacity, but it is far from being an intellectual exercise. Musical cerebration as a game for its own sake may fascinate a small minority of experts or specialists, but it has no true significance unless its rhythmic patterns and melodic designs, its harmonic tensions and expressive timbres penetrate the deepest layer of our subconscious mind. It is, in fact, the immediacy of this marriage of mind and heart, . . . that typifies the art of music and makes it different from all other arts.

Copland on Music, Aaron Copland. New York: Doubleday & Company, Inc., 1960, pp. 64–65.

GLOSSARY of musical terms used in *Music in Our Heritage*

Accelerando (accel.) Tempo gradually becoming faster

Adagio Slow; slower than *andante* and faster than *largo*. **Adagissimo** Extremely slow

Ad libitum (ad lib.) At will; according to the discretion of the performer

Alla breve Indicates that the written $\frac{4}{4}$ meter is to be interpreted as $\frac{2}{2}$; i.e., with the half note as the basic unit of time

Allegretto Tempo between *allegro* and *andante*

Allegrezza Liveliness

Allegro Quick, lively, cheerful

Andante Rather slow; moderately flowing

Andantino Quicker than *andante*

Animando Becoming more animated

Animé Animated, lively, spirited

Arco Play (a stringed instrument) with the bow. See *pizzicato*.

Aria In an opera, oratorio, or cantata, an extended song for solo voice, often a showpiece for the singer's vocal ability

Art song Song by a serious composer which strives for the maximum unity of text, vocal setting, and accompaniment. See pp. 72, 78, and 79.

Assai Very

Assez Enough; rather

Ballet Theatrical production (often narrative) centered on dance, generally with costumes, scenery, and orchestral music; or the music written for such a production

Bar Measure; the space on a staff between any two consecutive vertical lines (bar lines), comprising the number of beats indicated by the time signature

Ben Well

Blues One form of jazz, originating early in the 20th century, characterized by a 12-bar harmonic pattern, slow to moderate tempo, and the use of "blue notes," the flatted 3rd and 7th notes of the scale

Bolero Spirited Spanish dance in triple time, accompanied by castanets; Ravel uses characteristic rhythms in his *Bolero*.

Brio Vigor, spirit

Cadence Close; the harmonic progression and rhythmic punctuation used to end a musical phrase or section

Cadenza Passage in a brilliant, improvisatory style, often for display of a soloist's virtuosity

Canon Composition in which two or more voices have the same melody but enter in succession instead of simultaneously. See p. 70.

Cantabile In a singing style; smooth, expressive

Cantata Vocal composition of several movements for soloists and chorus, with either religious or secular text

Capriccioso Fanciful, capricious

Chamber music Music written for smaller groups than the large chorus or full orchestra, often having only one voice or instrument for each part, as a string quartet

Chantey English and American sailors' song, the rhythm of which helped co-ordinate movements of men working together

Chorale Congregational hymn of the German Lutheran Church. See p. 66.

Chord Three or more notes sounded together and written in vertical alignment; the basic unit of harmony

Coda "Tail"; a short section added at the end of a composition for a more effective close

Con With

Concerto (1) The *concerto grosso* of Bach's time, a composition, usually in three movements, contrasting a small group of solo instruments with the full orchestra, as Bach's Brandenburg Concerto No. 2. (2) Composition for a solo instrument with orchestra, usually in three movements, as Gershwin's Concerto in F for piano

Consonance Interval or chord that sounds "pleasant" or "at rest." This is a relative term, and each new musical era has generally heard more chords and intervals as consonant (or at least as less dissonant) than the last. See dissonance.

Contrapuntal Refers to a composition or passage written in counterpoint

Counterpoint Two or more independent melodic lines moving simultaneously, each designed to complement the other(s), usually by contrast in rhythm or direction (movement up or down) or both

Crescendo (cresc.) Growing louder

Da Capo al Fine (D.C. al Fine) Repeat from the beginning and continue to the word *Fine*

Dal Segno (D.S.) Repeat from the sign (:S:)

Diminuendo (dim.) Growing softer, diminishing

Discordant Dissonant; "unpleasant" (interval or chord). See dissonance and consonance.

Dissonance Interval or chord that sounds "unpleasant" and unstable, with a strong pull toward a consonance. See consonance and resolve.

Dolce Sweet, soft. **Dolcissimo** Very sweet and soft

Dynamics Different degrees of loudness and softness

E, Et And

8va Play an octave higher (if *8va* is above the staff) or lower (if *8va* is below) than written

Espressivo Expressive

Fantasia Free instrumental composition of improvisatory or imaginative character

227

Finale Last movement of a composition, such as a symphony or concerto, in several movements

Fine End

Folk song Song of unknown authorship which has for several generations or even centuries been current among (and characteristic of) the people of a nation or region

Form The basic design of a composition; the organization of musical principles (repetition, contrast, development, etc.) which determines the general framework of the composition

Forte (*f*) Loud, strong. **Fortissimo** (*ff*) Very loud

Fugue Composition in which a single subject (theme), announced alone in the beginning, is developed in contrapuntal, imitative style by three, four, or five voices (parts) of equal importance

Gavotte 17th- and 18th-century French dance, graceful and elegant, in duple time; often included in suites of that period, and "modernized" as the third movement of Prokofiev's Classical Symphony

Giusto Just, exact, proper

Glissando (**gliss.**) Scale passage performed in a rapid slide

G.P. General pause; a few beats' rest for the whole orchestra

Grandezza Grandeur, dignity

Grazioso Graceful

Harmony The relationships of notes within intervals and chords, and of successive intervals and chords to one another

Instrumentation See orchestration

Interval The distance in pitch between two notes sounded simultaneously or consecutively, or the two notes regarded as a unit. The number name of an interval (2nd, 3rd, etc.) is determined by the number of lines and spaces included by the two notes on the staff; the quality of the interval (perfect, major, minor, augmented, diminished) depends on the actual number of steps and half steps it includes.

Key The scale on which a composition is centered, as A major, F minor

Largo Very slow, broad, dignified

Legato Smooth, connected

Leggiero Light

Lent, Lento Slow

Ma, Mais But

Maestoso Majestic

Major Refers to: (1) a scale with half steps between the 3rd and 4th tones and the 7th and 8th tones, all other intervals being whole steps; (2) the key identified with such a scale; (3) a triad (three-note chord) with a lower interval of a major 3rd (two whole steps) and an upper interval of a minor 3rd (one and a half steps). See minor.

Manual Organ keyboard for the hands, as distinct from the pedals

Marcato Marked, accented

Mass The central service of the Roman Catholic liturgy; a musical setting of portions (the Ordinary) of the Mass

Melody Succession of single tones which together form a recognizable musical expression

Meno Less

Meter Design for grouping the rhythmic beats of a composition; indicated in written music by the meter signature, e.g., in $\frac{2}{4}$ meter the music is divided into measures of two beats each, a quarter note having the value of one beat

Metronome Mechanical device for demonstrating the exact tempo of a composition for which a metronome marking is provided. The number in a metronome marking indicates the number of beats per minute.

Mezzo (*m*) Half, medium, as in *mf, mp*, etc.

Minor Refers to: (1) a scale (a) with half steps between the 2nd and 3rd tones and the 5th and 6th tones, all other intervals being whole steps (natural form), (b) like the natural minor but with the 7th tone a half step higher (harmonic form), or (c) like the natural minor but with the 6th and 7th tones a half step higher in the ascending scale only (melodic form); (2) the key identified with such a scale; (3) a triad with a lower interval of a minor 3rd and an upper interval of a major 3rd. See major.

Minuet 17th- and 18th-century French dance, stately and graceful, in triple time; often included in suites, or adapted for the third movement of a symphony, sonata, etc.

Mode (1) One of the several medieval scales, each composed of a specific arrangement of steps and half steps. (2) Two of these modes, the Ionian and Aeolian, have survived to provide the pattern of steps and half steps in today's major and minor scales; hence we speak of the major and minor modes.

Moderatamente Moderately

Moderato, Modéré Moderate

Modo Manner, style

Modulate To change the tonal center, or key, within a composition

Molto Much, very

Mosso Moved

Moto Movement, motion

Movement Each of the smaller, self-contained sections (usually three or four) which together make up a symphony, concerto, string quartet, etc.

Muted The tone (of a stringed or brass instrument) softened by a special device

Nel In the

Nocturne Literally, "night" piece; generally, a Romantic mood piece

Non Not, no

Octave Interval of an 8th. An octave is the most consonant interval; any two notes an octave apart have the same pitch feeling.

Open Without mute

Opera Theatrical production which combines drama, vocal and orchestral music, costumes, scenery, and sometimes dance

Oratorio Musical drama for solo voices, chorus, and orchestra, usually based on a religious narrative but performed without scenery or action, as Handel's *Messiah*. See p. 82.

Orchestration Art of making effective use of individual instruments and groups of instruments in writing or arranging a composition for orchestra

Organum Earliest kind of part-writing, in which two melodic lines (voices) move together in parallel 4ths or 5ths, usually beginning and closing on the unison

Overture Orchestral introduction to an opera, play, etc., as Beethoven's Overture to *Egmont;* or an independent composition, as Brahms' *Tragic Overture*

Passacaglia Instrumental composition made up of variations on a short subject, which usually recurs in the bass

Passion Musical setting, for solo voices, chorus, and instruments, of the story of Christ's last days as told in one of the Gospels

Pavane 16th-century dance in duple time, courtly and grave; used by Ravel in his *Pavane pour une infante défunte*

Pedals (ped.) The organ keyboard played by the feet

Pentatonic scale Five-tone scale corresponding in the arrangement of intervals to the black keys of the piano (F#, G#, A#, C#, D#); found as the basis of much folk music throughout the world

Pesante Heavy, ponderous

Piano (p) Soft. **Pianissimo (pp)** Very soft

Più More

Pizzicato (pizz.) With the strings plucked with the fingers instead of bowed

Poco Little. **Poco a poco** Little by little

Polyphony Music consisting of two or more independent melodic lines sounding together. See counterpoint.

Polytonality Simultaneous use of two or more tonalities (keys) in a composition

Prelude (1) Musical introduction; before an opera, often using themes from the opera, as Wagner's Prelude to *Die Meistersinger von Nürnberg*. (2) Also applied to several different kinds of short pieces

Presto Very fast. **Prestissimo** As fast as possible

Programme Extra-musical inspiration for a descriptive or suggestive piece of music; also, the preface to a composition, in which the composer clarifies the extra-musical meaning of the work

Quintet Any composition for five instruments or voices, each having a separate part

Ragtime Form of jazz popular from about 1890 until World War I. Ragtime began as a style of piano writing characterized by embellishment and almost continuous syncopation; during its heyday it was an important influence on popular song writing.

Rallentando (rallent., rall.) Tempo gradually becoming slower

Recitativo Free passage, in the style of vocal declamation

Register Portion of the total range of a voice or instrument, as high, middle, or low register, each often having a particular quality

Requiem Musical setting of the Roman Catholic Mass for the Dead; many later compositions, such as Fauré's *Requiem* and Brahms' *German Requiem*, depart to a greater or lesser extent from the words of the liturgy and are performed only in concert.

Resolve In harmony, to move from a dissonance to a consonance toward which the former "pulls." See dissonance and consonance.

Rest Silence; or one of the symbols on the staff (each having a specific time value) used to indicate such a silence

Rhapsody Free fantasy, often of a brilliant, heroic, or emotional character

Rhythm Inclusive term dealing with all of the aspects of the flow of musical sound in time

Rinforzando (rf., rfz., rinfz.) Reinforced; with emphasis on a note or chord

Ritardando (rit.), Ritenuto (riten.) Holding back, slowing up

Rubato Deviation from strict tempo to enhance expression; free alternation of slight *accel.* and *rall.*

Rythmé Rhythmical

Scale Ascending or descending series of notes in a specific pattern of steps and half steps

Scherzino Playful, sportive

Scherzo Literally, "joke"; movement (usually the third) of a symphony, sonata, etc., characterized by rapid triple time, strongly (often unexpectedly) accented rhythms, and a quality of humor that may be capricious, whimsical, or sometimes grim

Score Musical notation of a composition, with each of the vocal and instrumental parts shown in vertical alignment. As a verb, *to score* means to orchestrate or arrange.

Sempre Always, continually

Senza Without

Serenade Originally, evening music for outdoor performance, often as a tribute; later used for songs, or compositions in several short movements for small instrumental groups, which retain the quality if not the function of early serenades

Sextet Any composition for six instruments or voices, each having a separate part

Sforzando (sf., sfz.) Forced; with a sudden, strong accent on a note or chord

Simile (sim.) Like; continue in like manner

Sinfonia Symphony

Solo Passage for single instrument or voice

Sonata Composition for one or two instruments, generally in three or four movements, the first often in sonata-allegro form

Sonata-allegro form The name for a general musical pattern consisting of three major divisions: Exposition, in which thematic elements (usually two main contrasting themes) and principal keys (again, usually two) are presented; Development, in which the thematic elements are treated in various ways and different keys are touched on or explored; and Recapitulation, a restatement of the Exposition with some modifications, mainly in the use of keys. A coda may be added.

Sostenuto Sustained

Spiritual Religious folk song of the American Negro, originating during the period of slavery

Staccato (**stacc.**; a dot over or under a note) Detached, separated; with the sounding time of each note shortened. **Staccatissimo** As detached as possible

Staff (**stave**) The five parallel horizontal lines, their pitch defined by a clef sign, on and between which musical notes are written

Stringendo Pressing; building up speed and excitement

String quartet Composition for two violins, viola, and cello, usually in several movements

Subito Sudden

Suite (1) In Bach's time, an instrumental composition in several short movements of dance character, as Bach's Orchestral Suites. (2) From the 19th century, any instrumental work of several short movements, often programmatic or descriptive, or excerpts from ballets, etc., as Debussy's *Suite bergamasque*

Symphony Large orchestral composition, generally in four contrasting movements, the first often in sonata-allegro form

Tanto So much

Tempo Time, rate of speed. **A Tempo** Return to original tempo

Tenuto (**ten.**) Sustained or slightly prolonged

Theme Musical idea, often made up of shorter figures or *motives*, recognizable as a prominent element in the structure of a composition; also called a subject

Toccata Literally, "touch" piece; a keyboard composition (16th – 18th century) generally intended as a showpiece for the capacities of the instrument and the virtuosity of the performer

Toujours Always, continually

Tranquillo Tranquil, calm

Transition Passage leading from one section of a composition to another, often involving harmonic modulation

Très Very

Trill (**tr.**) Rapid alternation of a given note and the one immediately above it

Trio (1) Any composition for three voices or instruments, each having a separate part. (2) Contrasting section between the first statement and the repetition of a minuet (or similar piece or movement)

Troppo Too much

Un A, an, one

Valse Waltz; a graceful, flowing 19th-century dance in triple time

Variations (**Theme and Variations**) Composition, each section of which is a different modification of the initial theme

Vif, Vivace, Vivo Lively, animated

Virtuoso Performer who is known for brilliant and dazzling displays of technical proficiency (virtuosity)

Whole-tone scale Scale of only six different tones, each separated by a whole step

CLASSIFIED INDEX TO VOCAL MUSIC

INDEX TO TWELVE FAMOUS COMPOSERS

MOZART, WOLFGANG AMADEUS
Time Line, 129
Symphony No. 40: Movement 1
Scored for Listening, 130
Scored for Singing, 134
Letters and Opinions, 206

MUSSORGSKY, MODEST
Time Line, 156
Pictures at an Exhibition
Scored for Listening, 157
Scored for Singing, 163
Letters and Opinions, 215

PROKOFIEV, SERGEI
Time Line, 183
Classical Symphony
Scored for Listening, 184
Scored for Singing, 192
Letters and Opinions, 221

RAVEL, MAURICE
Time Line, 172
String Quartet in F: Movement 2
Scored for Listening, 173
Scored for Singing, 176
Letters and Opinions, 218

STRAVINSKY, IGOR
Time Line, 177
Rite of Spring, The: Introduction, Dance
of the Youths and Maidens
Scored for Listening, 178
Scored for Singing, 182
Letters and Opinions, 219

WAGNER, RICHARD
Time Line, 141
Die Meistersinger von Nürnberg: Prelude
Scored for Listening, 142
Scored for Singing, 146
Letters and Opinions, 211

ALPHABETICAL AND ARRANGEMENT INDEX TO VOCAL MUSIC

In the chart below, the first column indicates the combination of voices for which each selection is arranged. If you wish to reduce the number of voice parts, consult columns 2 and 3. The piano accompaniment effectively completes the harmony of these alternate arrangements. Except for those selections marked *a cappella*, all arrangements are designed to be sung with accompaniment. Harmonies indicated by the chord symbols do not always coincide with the written accompaniment. For this reason it is suggested that improvised accompaniments be used for unison singing only. All of the arrangements in this book may be reduced to unison singing except those begining on pages 26, 67, 82, 89 and 149.

	Arrangement Classification	Reduced to Three Parts	Reduced to Two Parts
A la claire Fontaine (At the Fountain), 46	SAT		
All Round the Mountain, 6	SATB‡	SAT or STB	ST
America, 30	SATB°		
Andrea Chenier: Parting Chorus, 93	SSA		
Angelique-O, 50	SB		
Artsa alinu (Homeland), 45	SB		
Auprès de ma blonde, 43	SATB‡	SAT or SAB	ST
Babe of Bethlehem, The, 24	SAB		SB
Balm in Gilead, 21	SATB	SAT	ST
Bartered Bride, The: Opening Chorus, 91	SATB		
Blow the Wind Southerly, 35	SATB°	SAT	
Bonnie Doon, 34	SB		
Canon, Four Parts in One, 29	Canon°		
Christmas Oratorio: Praise Ye the Lord of Hosts, 82	SATB		
Dear Love, Now I Must Leave Thee, 64	SAB°		
Ein Ton (One Tone), 79	Unison		
Every Night When the Sun Goes In, 4	SB		
German Requiem: How Lovely Is Thy Dwelling Place, 149	SATB		
Give My Regards to Broadway, 110	SB		
Greensleeves, 42	SAB		SB or AB
Hello, My Baby, 106	Unison		
Henrietta's Wedding, 60	SATB	STB	ST
Hey, Look Me Over, 112	SB		

° — may be sung *a cappella*
‡ — chord symbols

233

	Arrangement Classification	Reduced to Three Parts	Reduced to Two Parts
Ich liebe dich (I Love You), 72	Unison		
I'm on My Way, 22	SATB°		
In the Gloaming, 103	SAB		SB
In the Good Old Summer Time, 107	SAB		SA
Johnny's My Boy, 63	Unison°		
Kanon, 71	Canon°		
Kitty Magee, 38	SAB‡		
Laredo, 57	SB		
Lenox, 26	SATB°		
Lonesome Dove, The, 15	Unison		
Lonesome Road, 8	SAB		SB
Madama Butterfly: Humming Chorus, 96	Unison		
Mary's a Grand Old Name, 109	SB		
Mass VII: Kyrie, 67	SATB°		
Masters in This Hall, 39	SATB		
Meeres-Stille (Sea Calm), 75	Unison		
Me Gustan Todas (I'm Fond of All Girls), 53	SB		
My Joy Would Grow in Measure, 48	Unison		
My Shepherd Will Supply My Need, 28	STB°		
Nelly Bly, 99	SB		
Night Bells, 87	SATB°		
Now the Day Is Over, 30	SATB°	SAT	SA
O God, Our Help in Ages Past, 31	SATB°		
Ole Buttermilk Sky, 115	SB		
Put On a Happy Face, 118	Unison		
Puttin' On the Style, 10	SB		
Requiem: Pie Jesu, 85	Unison		
Santy Anno, 14	STB		SB
Sea, The, 76	Unison		
Sentimental Journey, 120	SATB		SB
So Long, 12	SB		
Star-Spangled Banner, The, 32	SATB°		
Sylvie, 1	SAB‡		SB
Tambourine Dance, 56	Unison		
There's a Meeting Here Tonight, 18	SATB°‡		
There's Music in the Air, 100	TTBB	TTB	TT
Tod und Schlaf (Death and Sleep), 70	Canon°		
Wade in the Water, 19	SB		
Wait Till the Sun Shines, Nellie, 108	SAB°		AB
When Johnny Comes Marching Home, 102	Unison		
While Strolling Through the Park, 104	SB		
Whole World Lies in Shadows, The, 66	SATB°		
Young and Old, 89	SATB°		

° — may be sung *a cappella*
‡ — chord symbols